Rooftop Solar Panels

What are these panels?   ~~solar panels~~

What do they do?   ~~collect energy from sunlight~~

Why are they on the roof of the house?

What happens in the house because of these solar panels?

Academic Language Mastery

Volumes in the
Academic Language Mastery Series

Series Editor: Ivannia Soto

Academic Language Mastery:
Conversational Discourse
in Context

Jeff Zwiers
Ivannia Soto

CORWIN
A SAGE Publishing Company

A SAGE Publishing Company

FOR INFORMATION:

Corwin

A SAGE Company

2455 Teller Road

Thousand Oaks, California 91320

(800) 233-9936

www.corwin.com

SAGE Publications Ltd.

1 Oliver's Yard

55 City Road

London EC1Y 1SP

United Kingdom

SAGE Publications India Pvt. Ltd.

B 1/I 1 Mohan Cooperative Industrial Area

Mathura Road, New Delhi 110 044

India

SAGE Publications Asia-Pacific Pte. Ltd.

3 Church Street

#10-04 Samsung Hub

Singapore 049483

Printed in the United States of America

ISBN 978-1-5063-3801-9

This book is printed on acid-free paper.

Program Director: Dan Alpert

Senior Associate Editor: Kimberly Greenberg

Editorial Assistant: Katie Crilley

Production Editor: Amy Schroller

Copy Editor: Pam Schroeder

Typesetter: C&M Digitals (P) Ltd.

Proofreader: Dennis W. Webb

Indexer: Sheila Bodell

Cover Designer: Anupama Krishnan

Marketing Manager: Charline Maher

SUSTAINABLE FORESTRY INITIATIVE

Certified Chain of Custody

Promoting Sustainable Forestry

www.sfiprogram.org

SFI-01268

SFI label applies to text stock

16 17 18 19 20 10 9 8 7 6 5 4 3 2 1

Contents

Acknowledgments

I would like to acknowledge each of the authors who coauthored this series with me: Margarita Calderón, David and Yvonne Freeman, Noma LeMoine, and Jeff Zwiers. I have been inspired by each of your work for so long, and it was an honor learning and working with you on this project. I know that this book series is stronger due to each of your contributions and will therefore affect the lives of so many English language learners (ELLs) and SELs. Thank you for taking this journey with me on behalf of students who need our collective voices!

I would also like to acknowledge my editor, Dan Alpert, who has believed in me and has supported my work since 2008. Thank you for tirelessly advocating for equity, including language equity, for so long! Thank you also for advocating for and believing in the vision of the Institute for Culturally and Linguistically Responsive Teaching (ICLRT)!

Also to be thanked is Corwin, for supporting my work over time as well as early contributions to ICLRT. Corwin has grown over the time that I published my first book in 2009, but they still remain a family. I would especially like to thank Michael Soule, Lisa Shaw, Kristin Anderson, Monique Corrdiori, Amelia Arias, Taryn Waters, Charline Maher, Kim Greenberg, and Katie Crilley for each of your parts in making this book series and ICLRT a success!

Last, I would like to acknowledge the California Community Foundation, whose two-year grant assisted greatly with fully launching ICLRT at Whittier College. Thank you for believing that effective professional development over time can and will create achievement and life changes for ELLs and SELs!

—Ivannia Soto

PUBLISHER'S ACKNOWLEDGMENTS

Corwin gratefully acknowledges the contributions of the following reviewers:

Bridget Erickson
Teacher, Literacy Specialist
Oakwood Elementary School,
Wayzata Public Schools
Plymouth, MN

Norma Godina-Silva
Education Coach and
    Consultant
Preeminence ELL Resources
    and Solutions, Inc.
El Paso, TX

Katherine Lobo
ESL Teacher, President of
    MATSOL
Newton South High School
Newton, MA

Jill Manning
LAUSD
Los Angeles, CA

Betsy Rogers
2003 National Teacher of the
    Year
Department Chair, and
    Assistant Professor
    of Curriculum and
    Instruction
Samford University
Birmingham, AL

Tonya Ward Singer
Author and Consultant
Santa Rosa, CA

Bonnie Tryon
Mentor and Coach
School Administrators
    Association of New York
    State (SAANYS)
Cobleskill, NY

About the Authors

Dr. Jeff Zwiers is a senior researcher at the Stanford Graduate School of Education and director of professional development for the Understanding Language Initiative, a research and professional learning project focused on improving the education of academic English learners. He has consulted for national and international teacher development projects that promote literacy, lesson design, and formative assessment practices. He has published articles and books on literacy, cognition, discourse, and academic language. His current research focuses on improving professional learning models and developing classroom instruction that fosters high-quality oral language and constructive conversations across disciplines.

Dr. Ivannia Soto is associate professor of education at Whittier College, where she specializes in second language acquisition, systemic reform for ELLs, and urban education. She began her career in the Los Angeles Unified School District (LAUSD), where she taught English and English language development to a population made up of 99.9 percent Latinos, who either were or had been ELLs. Before becoming a professor, Dr. Soto also served LAUSD as a literacy coach and district office administrator. She has presented on literacy and language topics at various conferences, including the National Association for Bilingual Education (NABE), the California Association for Bilingual Education (CABE), the American Educational Research Association (AERA), and the National Urban Education Conference.

As a consultant, Soto has worked with Stanford University's School Redesign Network (SRN) and WestEd as well as a variety of districts and county offices in California, providing technical assistance for systemic reform for ELLs and Title III. Soto is the co-author of *The Literacy Gaps: Building Bridges for ELLs and SELs* as well as author of *ELL Shadowing as a Catalyst for Change* and *From Spoken to Written Language With ELLs,* all published by Corwin. Together, the books tell a story of how to systemically close achievement gaps with ELLs by increasing their oral language production in academic areas. Soto is executive director of the Institute for Culturally and Linguistically Responsive Teaching (ICLRT) at Whittier College, whose mission it is to promote relevant research and develop academic resources for ELLs and SELs via linguistically and culturally responsive teaching practices.

Series Dedication

I dedicate this book series to the teachers and administrators in Whittier Union High School District (WUHSD). WUHSD has been a pivotal learning partner with ICLRT over the past four years. By embedding ICLRT Design Principles and academic language development (ALD) best practices into their teaching and professional development, they have fully embraced and worked tirelessly in classrooms to meet the needs of ELLs and SELs. Specifically, I would like to thank Superintendent Sandy Thorstenson, Assistant Superintendent Loring Davies, and ELL Director Lilia Torres-Cooper (my high school counselor and the person who initially brought me into WUHSD) as well as ALD Certification teachers Diana Banzet, Amy Cantrell, Carlos Contreras, Carmen Telles Fox, Nellie Garcia, Kristin Kowalsky, Kelsey McDonnell, Damian Torres, and Heather Vernon, who have committed themselves fully to this work. I would also like to thank Lori Eshilian, principal of Whittier High School (my high school alma mater), for being willing to do whatever it takes to meet the needs of all students, including partnering with ICLRT on several projects over the past few years. You were my first and best physical education teacher and have modeled effective collaboration since I was in high school!

—Ivannia Soto, Series Editor

Book Dedication

I would like to dedicate this book to the many teachers who are constantly thinking about how to best meet their students' many needs, striving to become the most effective teachers they can be in a variety of challenging school settings.

—Jeff Zwiers

CHAPTER ONE

Introduction to the Book Series

According to the Migration Policy Institute (2013), close to 5 million U.S. students, which represent 9 percent of public school enrollment, are English language learners (ELLs). Three-quarters of these 5 million students were born in the United States and are either the children or grandchildren of immigrants. In some large urban school districts such as Los Angeles, ELLs already comprise around 30 percent of the student population. These demographic trends, along with the rigorous content expectations of new content and language standards (e.g., CCSS, WIDA, ELPA21, etc.), require that educational systems become skilled at simultaneously scaffolding academic language and content for this growing group of students. For ELLs, academic language mastery is the key to accessing rigorous content. Now is a pivotal time in educational history to address both academic language and content simultaneously so that ELLs do not fall further behind in both areas while also becoming bored by methods that are cognitively banal and lead to disengagement.

Another group of students who have academic language needs, but are not formally identified as such, are standard English learners (SELs). SELs are students who speak languages that do not correspond to standard American English language structure and grammar but incorporates English vocabulary. They include African American students who speak African American language (AAL), sometimes referred to as African American English, and

Mexican American–non-new-immigrant students who speak Mexican American Language (MxAL) or what is commonly referred to as "Chicano English." ELLs and SELS also need instructional assistance in the academic language necessary to be successful in school, college, and beyond. For both groups of students, academic language represents the pathway to full access in meeting the rigorous demands of the new standards.

Purpose of This Academic Language Development Book Series

The purpose of this series is to assist educators in developing expertise in, and practical strategies for, addressing four key dimensions of academic language when working with ELLs and SELs. To systemically address the needs of ELLs and SELs, we educators must share a common understanding of academic language development (ALD). Wong-Fillmore (2013) defines academic language as "the language of texts. The forms of speech and written discourse that are linguistic resources educated people in our society can draw on. This is language that is capable of supporting complex thought, argumentation, literacy, successful learning; it is the language used in written and spoken communication in college and beyond" (p. 15). Given that we are preparing ELLs and SELs for college, career, and beyond, they should receive ample opportunities to learn and use academic language, both in spoken and written form (Soto, 2014). ELLs and SELs also must be provided with scaffolded access to cognitively and linguistically demanding content, which allows them to cultivate their complex thinking and argumentation.

All students can benefit from academic language development modeling, scaffolding, and practice, but ELLs and SELs need it to survive and thrive in school. ELLs have plenty of language assets in their primary language that we must leverage to grow their academic English, yet there is often a very clear language and literacy gap that must be closed as soon as ELLs enter school. Similarly, SELs come to school with a language variation that, to be built upon in the classroom setting, must first be understood. In reviewing the wide range of literature by experts in this field, most agree that the key elements of academic English language for ELLs and SELs include these four dimensions: academic vocabulary, syntax and grammar, discourse, and culturally responsive teaching.

We have therefore organized this book series around these four dimensions of academic English:

- Conversational Discourse—developing students' conversational skills as an avenue for fostering academic language and thinking in a discipline
- Academic Vocabulary—teaching high-frequency academic words and discipline-specific vocabulary across content areas
- Syntax and Grammar—teaching sophisticated and complex syntactical and grammatical structures in context
- Culturally Responsive Teaching—incorporating culture while addressing and teaching language and honoring students' home cultures and communities

The focus on these four dimensions in this book series makes this a unique offering for educators. By building upon the cultural and linguistic similarities of ELLs and SELs, we embed strategies and instructional approaches about academic vocabulary, discourse, and grammar and syntax within culturally responsive teaching practices to make them all accessible to teachers of diverse students. As the American poet and great thinker of modern Hispanic literature, Sabine Ulibarrí, noted, "Language is culture; it carries with it traditions, customs, the very life of a people. You cannot separate one from the other. To love one is to love the other; to hate one is to hate the other. If one wants to destroy a people, take away their language and their culture will soon disappear." Therefore, the heart of this book series is integrating language, culture, and content in a manner that has not been addressed with other books or book series on ALD.

ACADEMIC LANGUAGE DEVELOPMENT DIMENSIONS DEFINED AND CONNECTIONS TO THE BOOK SERIES

ALD is a pathway to equity. With new rigorous state standards and expectations, ALD provides access for ELLs and SELs so that high academic expectations can be maintained and reached. The following matrix defines each dimension of ALD and demonstrates the connection of that dimension across the book series. For full proficiency in ALD, it is integral that each dimension be addressed across disciplines—the dimensions should not be taught as either/ or skills. Instead, each of the dimensions should be addressed throughout a course of study or unit. In that way, it is important to read the book series in its entirety, as an ongoing professional development growth tool (more on that later). The matrix also demonstrates the connections made between ALD dimensions, which will prove helpful as readers complete continue their study across the ALD book series.

ALD Dimension	Definition	Connections to the Book Series
Conversational Discourse	Conversational discourse is the language (words sentences, and organizational strategies, etc.) used to co-consruct complex ideas with others. The essential components of conversational discourse include: • Clarifying and negotiating the meaning of words and sentences. • Supporting ideas with reasons and evidence • Evaluating evidence and choosing the "strongest" ones. • Adding new information to build on the ideas of a partner • Staying focused on the topic of the conversation	• Conversational discourse involves the overlap of academic vocabulary (words) and many of the components also often associated with academic reading and writing across genres (organization, text structure, purpose, and audience). This book addresses a specific form of discourse, conversational discourse, and its specific conversational skills.
Academic Vocabulary	Words are separate units of information; it is tempting to focus on them as "pieces of knowledge" to accumulate to show learning. Instead, words should be tools and materials for constructing more complete and complex messages. In this book series, we will focus on Tier 2 (high-frequency words that go across content areas) and Tier 3	Academic vocabulary is associated with the density of words used in academic discourse as well as the use of connectives and transitions used in grammar.

ALD Dimension	Definition	Connections to the Book Series
Academic Vocabulary, continued	(abstract or nuanced words that exist within a particular content area or discipline) academic vocabulary.	
Grammar and Syntax in Context	Academic language is characterized by technical vocabulary, lexical density, and abstraction. Academic genres have predictable components, cohesive texts, and language structures that include nominalizations, passives, and complex sentences.	ELLs and SELs need to engage in academic discourse in the classroom and develop academic vocabulary. These are essential building blocks for learning to read and write cohesive texts using academic genres and the language structures characteristic of academic language.
Culturally and Linguistically Responsive Practices	Culturally responsive pedagogy incorporates high-status, accurate cultural knowledge about different ethnic groups into all subjects and skills taught. It validates, facilitates, liberates, and empowers ethnically diverse students by simultaneously cultivating their cultural integrity, individual abilities, and academic success (Gay, 2000)	ELLs and SELs are more likely to acquire ALD when they are viewed from an asset model and when ALD is taught as associated with concepts that connect to their cultural knowledge. This book will address linguistic diversity, including variations of English.

(Definitions adapted from Academic Language Development Network (n.d.) *unless otherwise noted)*

FORMAT FOR EACH BOOK

At the beginning of each book is an introduction to the purpose of the book series, including the format of each book and their intersections. Additionally, connections between current ALD research and the specific dimension of ALD are included in an abbreviated literature review. In the middle of each book, the voice of the expert in the particular ALD dimension is incorporated with practical strategies and classroom examples. These chapters include how to move from theory to practice, classroom examples at elementary and secondary levels, and ways to assess the dimension. At the end of each book, a summary of major points and how to overcome related challenges are included along with the rationale for use of the Institute for Culturally and Linguistically Responsive Teaching (ICLRT) Design Principles as a bridge between ALD and content. Also included at the end of each book are additional professional development resources.

Additionally, each book in the series is organized in a similar manner for ease of use by the reader. Chapter 1 is the introduction to the series of books, and not an introduction for each individual book. Instead, Chapter 2 introduces each dimension of ALD with the specific research base for that book. The heart of each book in the series is in Chapter 3, where practical application to theory and classroom examples can be found. Chapter 4 addresses how each ALD dimension fosters literacy development. In Chapter 5, how to assess the specific ALD dimension is discussed with checklists and rubrics to assist with formative assessment in this area. Last, Chapter 6 connects each volume with the others in the series and details how the book series can best be used in a professional development setting. The epilogue provides a description of the relationship to the underlying principles of the ICLRT.

- Chapter 1—Introduction to the Book Series
- Chapter 2—What Research Says About Conversational Discourse
- Chapter 3—Classroom Applications for Conversational Discourse
- Chapter 4—Learning From Classroom Examples of Conversational Discourse
- Chapter 5—Assessing Conversational Discourse
- Chapter 6—Conclusions, Challenges, and Connections

HOW TO USE THE BOOK SERIES

While each book can stand alone, the book series was designed to be read together with colleagues and over time. As such, it is a professional development tool for educational communities, which can also be used for extended learning on ALD. Educators may choose to begin with any of the four key dimensions of ALD that interests them the most or with which they need the most assistance.

How to Use Reflect and Apply Queries

Embedded throughout this book series you will find queries that will ask you to reflect and apply new learning to your own practice. Please note that you may choose to use the queries in a variety of settings either with a book study buddy or during PLC, grade-level, or department meetings. Each of the queries can be answered in a separate journal while one is reading the text, or as a group you may choose to reflect on only a few queries throughout a chapter. Please feel free to use as many or as few queries as are helpful to you, but we do encourage you to at least try a couple out for reflection as you read the book series.

Try it out by responding to the first query here.

REFLECT AND APPLY

What does this Sabine Ulibarrí quote mean to you? How does it connect to your students?

"Language is culture; it carries with it traditions, customs, the very life of a people. You cannot separate one from the other. To love one is to love the other; to hate one is to hate the other. If one wants to destroy a people, take away their language and their culture will soon disappear."

Book Series Connection to Conversational Discourse

Conversational Discourse is an essential dimension of ALD. Often, however, educators may be reluctant to make space for student talk in the classroom for fear of losing control of classroom management or because they primarily had examples of teacher or professor talk throughout their own schooling and/or teacher education programs. In her latest book, *A House of My Own: Stories of My Life*, Chicana author Sandra Cisneros (2015) shares the following about speaking in school, "At home I was fine, but at school I never opened my mouth except when the teacher called on me. . . . I didn't like school because all they saw was the outside of me."

Many teachers have brilliant students such as Cisneros in our classrooms but may not know it because we may not have created spaces for all students to voice their ideas and develop their academic identities in our classrooms. Instead, classroom talk is an opportunity for students to build and create a community within the classroom setting, especially when learners interact with colleagues from varying abilities and backgrounds. In this way, students and teachers can begin to understand not just the "outside" of one another, but the "inside" as well, because multiple perspectives are shared, heard, and valued during structured classroom talk.

Many teachers have already begun their journeys into rich classroom discourse using small groups or Think-Pair-Shares, and they are now ready to take academic oral language to the next level. Research on second language acquisition suggests that a major foundation of literacy is academic oral language. Unfortunately, many teachers think that oral language is static or that it's too late to develop it. On the contrary, it is vital for students, ELLs, and SELs in particular, to practice academic oral language in classroom settings, especially when this is the only place that many students will hear academic language models.

The approaches introduced in this book in the series, along with the ICLRT Design Principles, provide a theoretical and practical framework for addressing ALD in a contextualized manner and across disciplines. This short (teachers are busy people) book builds teachers' knowledge and confidence with respect to the core conversational skills that can be used in lessons to extend academic oral language practice and foster communication skills.

CHAPTER TWO

What Research Says About Conversational Discourse

"It is easy to imagine talk in which ideas are explored rather than answers to teachers' test questions provided and evaluated; in which teachers talk less than the usual two-thirds of the time and students talk correspondingly more; in which students themselves decide when to speak rather than waiting to be called on by the teacher; and in which students address each other directly. Easy to imagine, but not easy to do." —Courtney Cazden (2001)

A cademic language is a lot like an ocean. We have a much better idea of its surface features and the things that swim around near the top, but go a little deeper and things get murky. You can't clearly define academic language, and it's always changing. And yet, it is the deeper and murkier depths of language use that can make the biggest differences in student success, both positive and negative. Students can be overwhelmed by it and struggle to survive in school and career, or they can use it like a submarine that rides its currents and diversity to succeed in academic life and beyond.

It might also help to have a less metaphorical working definition. For now, let's use this one: Academic language is the language used for describing the thinking skills, complex processes, and abstract ideas that are valued in school. This definition, of course, covers an extremely wide range of words, sentences, paragraphs, and ways of putting them together to communicate academic ideas.

9

In recent decades, numerous resources and ideas have emerged for developing students' academic language and literacy across disciplines. Common strategies include "explicit" teaching of academic vocabulary and grammar, sentence frames, analysis of text features, "close" reading, graphic organizers, computer-based reading programs, and more. Whereas most of these can and do play roles in developing academic language, this book zooms in on a less common and, to be honest, more challenging approach for fostering academic language: conversation.

Many of our students have been labeled according to their language abilities. These include: English ELLs learners, most of whom were not raised in English-speaking homes; long-term ELLs, who have been in U.S. schools for more than four years and are not as proficient as they should be; SELs, who grew up speaking variations of English that do not heavily overlap with the language used for school tasks; and fluent English speakers, who benefit greatly from the aforementioned overlap. Yet it is more accurate to say that every student is on a variety of continuums of English proficiency. A student might be higher on the reading continuum than speaking or lower on the listening continuum than on the writing one. A student might be higher on the science language continuum than on the history continuum, lower on the math continuum than the English one, and so on. The power of using conversations is that all students, regardless of where they are on the continuums, can benefit from talking with others.

LANGUAGE ACQUISITION RESEARCH

Let's start by digging into the research foundations for language acquisition. First, second, and academic language acquisition are not the same, but they do have several key dimensions in common. Picture a 2-year old with his mother at the zoo, an American college student in Rome with his Italian girlfriend, and a high school summer intern working at a physics laboratory. Odds are very high that all three learners will learn first, second, and academic languages quite well. Why? Because they want to and need to—especially the college student—to connect with others and do things with ideas in each setting.

In all three cases (first, second, and academic), we seldom know exactly when the person acquires a certain word, grammar skill, or conversation skill. Language learning is, in a nutshell, the result of immersion in messy and meaningful communication over time. A 2-year old wants to have something and tries out different ways to ask for it; the fifth-grade English learner has many conversations at lunch with fluent speakers; and the high school native English speaker (an academic EL) reads, writes, listens to, and speaks increasingly academic words and phrases over time, both at home and at school. All of these experiences push, in a good way, these learners' minds to expand and deepen how they can use language to understand and explain ideas.

Three dimensions contribute to language acquisition. The first is input (Krashen, 1985). This input, often in the form of listening or reading, needs to be comprehensible for the brain to be able to process it to make meaning. As meaning is made, the words and grammar begin to stick in the brain. As a person receives more similar input, the aspects of language used in the input are reinforced and stick even more. Another key dimension is output (Swain, 2000), which is usually in the form of speaking and writing. Output challenges the brain to put ideas into words and sentences that others can understand. It pushes a learner to try new ways of constructing and clarifying messages. As the learner succeeds in communicating meaning to others, the language used tends to stick. And the third dimension is interaction or conversation (Long, 1996). Interaction often includes lots of speaking and listening but also includes a wide range of communication skills that just input and output alone don't foster.

Students have had a fair amount of input in school in the forms of listening to teachers and reading texts, and they have produced a fair amount of output in school in the forms of speaking and writing. Granted, we can improve in our teaching all of these, but what we haven't done much of is work on helping students have rich peer-to-peer interactions, particularly in the form of extended conversations among students. One purpose of this book, in fact, is to describe the value of conversations—why they are worth precious class time—as well as how to use them in classroom settings to develop academic discourse skills and literacy.

CONVERSATIONAL DISCOURSE

The word *discourse* is commonly used in academic texts and presentations, but what is it, really? Like academic language, it has multiple overlapping meanings. Here we don't attempt to define it but instead present several terms that most often emerge in discourse's wide range of definitions in the literature: *extended, communication, discussion, argument, orderly, formal, reasoning, conversation, social practice, beyond the sentence level, how language is used in a discipline,* and *language in use.* These terms cover a lot of ground, so we have chosen to focus on one area under discourse's broad umbrella: conversation.

Thus, this book focuses on what we call *conversational discourse,* which is the use of language for extended, back-and-forth, and purposeful communication among people. Whereas this type of discourse can and does happen through the use of visual and written messages, we highlight oral conversations in this book. And we zoom in even further to focus on paired conversations because of the high concentration of listening and talking per minute that they offer to each student.

A key feature of conversational discourse is that it is used to create and clarify knowledge, not just transmit it. Too many people view language as just as a tool for transmission and reception of static ideas and knowledge. Language is not one solid tool but a dynamic and evolving mix of resources and flexible tools used to communicate, build, and choose ideas at any given moment. Conversation, as Theodore Zeldin (1998) writes, "is a meeting of minds with different memories and habits. When minds meet, they don't just exchange facts: they transform them, reshape them, draw different implications from them, engage in new trains of thought. Conversation doesn't just reshuffle the cards; it creates new ones."

THE CLASH OF LEARNING PARADIGMS

In recent decades, policies and testing practices have had a large influence on what learning looks like and how it is fostered. Especially in schools with diverse populations, huge emphasis was placed on choosing right answers on tests and raising test scores. Curricula, lessons, and classroom assessments were tailored to help students do well on these high-stakes tests. Learning, in the eyes of many students, teachers, and curriculum guides, meant memorizing word meanings, grammar rules, and the easiest-to-assess standards. Too many students have come to think that learning equals amassing points, which come from getting answers right on homework, quizzes, and tests. This is much like Paolo Freire's (1970) "banking model" of education in which teachers are supposed to deposit learning into student's passive minds.

Many educators are now working hard to move beyond this "memorize-for-points," quantity-focused paradigm of learning that still shapes instruction. This paradigm is deep-rooted because of the large amount of time it has been in place. Many teachers currently in the workforce were students in schools—and then teachers in training—under this paradigm. Moreover, the recent pushes for "data-driven" practices and spreadsheet-based results also tend to favor the quantity-focused paradigm. The messier collaboration-focused "quality" paradigm struggles to win in such a battle. We hope that this book will help to strengthen this messier, yet deeper, paradigm and also describe how to effectively assess growth along the way.

CONVERSATIONAL PURPOSES, MAXIMS, AND DISPOSITIONS

In an effective conversation, the participants, for the most part, have an agreed-upon purpose for talking with one another. Yet, many students don't know what the purpose of conversing is. Indeed, purposes beyond "to get points" are often lacking in school activities, including conversations. Students might view conversation as free time, a time to share or get answers, show off, and so on, but too many students don't see conversation as a chance to clarify and fortify ideas with another person or to engage in collaborative argumentation to make an important decision about an issue.

A foundational principle for any effective conversation is cooperation (Grice, 1975). This principle, called the cooperative principle, depends on several maxims (often called Grice's maxims), summarized here:

- Make your contribution not more or less informative than is required at the current stage of the conversation.
- Don't say ideas that you think are false or ideas that lack evidence.
- Be clear.
- Be relevant to the current stage of the conversation.

These maxims seem obvious at first, but upon closer inspection of them—and of typical conversations in classrooms—we see how important they are. Many students still need to learn how much they need to share, how to use evidence to shore up their ideas, what it means to be clear to different conversation partners, and how conversations work.

It also helps students to have certain interactional mind-sets, or dispositions, as they enter into conversations. These dispositions help to extend and enrich conversations. We have turned these into several "I will try" statements for students (many adults should try these, too). Look at each one, and consider what happens in a conversation if one or both partners don't have that particular disposition.

- I will try to help my partner think more deeply about this topic.
- I will try to allow my partner to help me think more deeply about this topic.
- I will try to understand this topic better during our conversation.
- I will try to work with my partner, not against, even if we disagree at times.
- I will try to be open to learning new ideas and having my ideas change.

Of course, in the messy world of real discourse—especially student discourse—we will see a wide range of quality when looking at the purposes, maxims, and dispositions in conversations. This is due, in part, to the overall expectations that students have about learning and about the role of discourse. If students have been conditioned over many years to think of learning as memorizing answers, then suddenly having them "think together" (Mercer, 2000) with others to build or negotiate ideas can clash with their theories of how they learn. This is a major shift in instruction and assessment that, in the minds and practices of both students and teachers, will take lots of work, time, and patience. Another shift is from a focus on self to more focus on others. Students should have in mind that they are not just in school for themselves but also to help others grow academically and socially. Most big assessments don't promote this view, but our daily lessons must do so if our students are to succeed in being collaborative members of society.

Students need teachers with a working knowledge of the many things that make classroom conversations effective, such as their purposes, prompts, maxims, dispositions, and skills. And students need hefty amounts of conversational experiences to maximize these things. But how do students learn, for example, how much information is typically required in a conversation, or how much evidence is needed to warrant sharing an idea, or what it means to be clear to peers who aren't friends, or what it means to share relevant information at the right times in a conversation? They need teachers who draw attention to these things, model them, and provide loads of practice and support throughout the year.

BUILDING IDEAS WITH THE "GIVEN" AND THE "NEW"

Now let's zoom in a bit to look at the more intricate gears of conversations. Most partner turns include two parts: the "given and the new" (Halliday & Matthiessen, 2013). The given is a mention of things already talked about. It might be a paraphrase, a recap, or a zooming in on information just shared in the conversation. It might be a reference to common knowledge or something experienced by both partners before this conversation. For ELLs, the given information is familiar, allowing them to more easily process the language used to describe it.

The "new" within a turn is information that is new to the conversation. Why talk if nothing new results? The new is usually connected to the purpose of a conversation and is vital for the building of ideas. Participants benefit from understanding and articulating new ideas, variations, perspectives, and so on. For ELLs, the generating and understanding of new ideas pushes them to use new language. Notice the given and the *new* in the following conversation:

(1) Bijila: All that gold? I think I would *buy a big house give some money to friends.*

(2) Manny: Yeah. Me too. Maybe *buy a nice car or jet plane. Maybe I could buy the school and make them give me good grades.*

(3) Bijila: *I don't think* they would do that. *You could give them money to buy new stuff, like desks and science stuff.*

(4) Manny: No, I don't know. Maybe. *But I'll leave school cuz I never gotta work, and/*

(5) Bijila: */But then you don't learn things for life. School is not just for jobs.* <u>So you get the gold, and buy a house, and what,</u> *watch TV all day?*

(6) Manny: Yeah.

(7) Bijila: <u>What about doing good, like the teacher said, with it?</u> *I want to give it to friends and maybe to buy like food for hungry people in other countries. I might/*

(8) Manny: */Maybe to some to friends and to my uncle but not my cousins. They're lame.*

Think about how this conversation and others like it can shape students' language and thinking. Both students are engaged in trying to go beyond just the givens and build new ideas. New ideas might include new ways to harness energy, solve a geometry problem, view a historical person, learn from a character in a story, and so on. Student minds have a need to go beyond the givens to connect, create, choose, and improve their lives and the world around them. As they push themselves to clarify given ideas and describe new ones, students push themselves to understand and use increasingly academic language.

CHOOSING THE BEST THING TO SAY NEXT

With few exceptions, each turn in a conversation is spontaneous. It depends on the previous turns and the current development of the ideas in the conversation. Thus, several conversations could start with the same initial idea, but given the amount of choices and "avenues" that keep branching off each with each turn, the conversations will likely diverge significantly.

Let's say you are in the middle of a conversation with one other person. Out of many possible things to say in your next turn, what is the best thing to say to realize the purpose(s) of the conversation? Although there are many choices, some are more likely than others to help the conversation along. There is never one "right" thing to say, of course, but as you learn more about conversations, you will see that some moves have more potential than others to realize their academic purposes, foster disciplinary thinking, and cultivate language.

As you are listening to your partner's current turn, you are doing several things in your mind. You are thinking about what new things he or she is adding and how well you understand what your partner is saying. You are thinking about what has been said so far in this conversation, what you already know about the topic, and what questions you might ask. You are thinking about what you might say next to build on your partner's current turn and how to make what you say as clear as possible. Other types of responses might also be emerging in your mind, such as encouraging your partner to clarify or support ideas, paraphrasing what your partner said to see if you understood, adding details or examples, evaluating evidence, negotiating, and respectfully challenging what your partner said. There are many others, but these moves, which are described in more detail in Chapter 3, are most of the most-likely-to-be-effective options in classroom conversations.

THE EFFECT OF CONVERSATIONAL DISCOURSE

So, what effect does conversational discourse have on students? Students' language, literacy, and thinking develop as a result of academically rich conversations that include the things described in this chapter. Content understandings and skills also develop. On a wider scale, the world becomes a better place because all of our students are becoming better prepared to engage in rich conversations with each other and future people with whom they interact in their colleges and careers. The next chapter describes these effects in more detail and how they can be leveraged in classroom settings.

REFLECT AND APPLY

1. How do you think conversations have influenced your knowledge, thinking, and language?

2. Why is conversational discourse rare in many classrooms?

3. Use this chapter to create a checklist of the features that you would like to see and hear in your students' conversations. Observe several conversations, and consider the features that are in most need of development.

CHAPTER THREE

Classroom Applications for Conversational Discourse

"The more genuine conversation is, the less its conduct lies within the will of either partner. . . . A conversation has a spirit of its own, and the language in which it is conducted bears its own truth within it—i.e., that it allows something to 'emerge' which hence forth exists." —Hans Georg Gadamer (1976)

Our brains thrive on creating ideas with others. Likewise, our ideas thrive when they are fed and challenged by conversation. And as Gadamer's quotation suggests, good conversations have their own spirits, cultivating ideas that go beyond the sum of what individual partners contribute. Unexpected thinking happens, new ideas emerge and, as a result, new ways of using language. Notice what emerges in the following conversation after students read a short story about a girl who faces various trials to buy skates and difficult practice sessions to prepare for the upcoming competition.

(1) Javier: What do you think the story teach us?

(2) Ruth: Maybe like try hard.

(3) Javier: Why?

(4) Ruth: To be good.

(5) Javier: I mean, why do you think that's the theme?

(6) Ruth: Oh. Cuz in the book she practice a lot to get good. At night, in cold and dark. She wants to/

(7) Javier: /And she save money to buy patines (skates).

(8) Ruth: Yeah, but for us? We don't skate.

(9) Javier: I don't know. Try hard to be good in soccer, maybe.

(10) Ruth: And school, too. Like study at night and not watch TV.

(11) Javier: And maybe to be good at life.

(12) Ruth: What do you mean?

(13) Javier: To be a good person. To be nice to everyone. Like you should/

(14) Ruth: /Even to mean people?

(15) Javier: Yeah. Some maybe they're mean cuz we aren't nice to them.

Notice how the idea of being nice to people evolves in the conversation. It is likely that neither student planned on coming up with this idea; it sprouted from the cross-pollination of ideas and their brains' natural push to create in collaboration with others.

Also notice that there isn't a lot of what is typically considered academic language in this conversation. This is OK. These two students are pushing themselves to think abstractly, interpret complex text, use evidence, and apply ideas to new contexts. These skills, for the moment, are more important than using academic vocabulary and grammar in their sentences. Indeed, in many cases when teachers impose language frames on students, conversation is stilted and often stalls. Students need the freedom to engage with each other and get excited about the new ideas that emerge in whatever language they have. Academic language will develop over time as students immerse themselves in academic texts and conversations based on them.

As we saw in Chapter 2, conversational discourse is messy business. Classroom conversations are all different, changing by the hour and impossible to grasp at any given moment. They are highly contextual and often are just snippets of "long conversations"

(Mercer, 2000) that last weeks, months, or even years. It is a lot easier to have students wade through the shallow waters of memorizing short answers, word meanings, and grammar rules than it is to explore and work in the murky depths of conversational discourse. Despite the messiness and challenges, we do know that engaging in a wide range of conversations like the ones in this book is necessary for students' academic development (Baker, Jensen, & Kolb, 2002). Language was invented to get useful things done and to be meaningful to its users. Going through the motions of communication doesn't stimulate the brain.

In an effective conversation, participants each bring valuable things to the table to share, whether they are initially cognizant of it or not. They listen and talk to achieve some purpose. The conversation is not an interview or a case of one person teaching another all there is to know about a topic. It is not a memorized dialog or a set of sentence frames to script every turn. Conversations are back-and-forth interactions in which participants build on one another's ideas to build up ideas that weren't in their minds before talking.

THE BENEFITS OF CONVERSATIONAL DISCOURSE

In each conversation, you get the benefits of frequent input and output, which as highlighted in Chapter 2 are vital for language development. Every other turn, your partner provides input. It might be short or long, but your brain has to process it as part of the larger conversation. This is a little like practicing to be a good tennis player. If you just use a machine that hurls the ball to the same spot every time, you get limited practice in returning the many types of shots you will need against a real opponent. But in frequently playing real people, your body needs to return a wide range of short and long forehand and backhand shots. And similar to shots in tennis, in conversation you often predict what the partner will say next and then confirm or change this prediction as your partner talks. The more often you talk with others, the better at predicting—and being ready to respond—you get. All of this demands extra thinking and processing of language.

Every other turn, you need to talk or respond in some way. You must quickly respond to what your partner said by putting your thought(s) into words and sentences. This frequent practice helps students develop their language "muscles" and communication "dexterity." Have you ever been exhausted after a rich conversation? Conversations, especially in pairs, are unique in that they allow little rest from thinking; you can't really space out or daydream when you have to think about what you are listening to and then think about what you will say in response to what your partner just said—and how you will say it—all the while thinking about the overall direction of the conversation.

Valuable Mini-Challenges in Each Turn

There are also many mini-challenges to overcome in each conversation. When one partner, let's call her Ana, wants to articulate an important idea to her partner, David, who doesn't know what will be said, there is a slight feeling of tension, or mini-challenge, that comes from wanting to communicate but not being exactly sure how. This mini-challenge is sometimes visible when a person pauses, looks off to the side, and thinks about how to say something. Ana, for example, must spontaneously combine words, sentences, and other nonverbal cues to get her new idea across while also reading David's cues for how well he is understanding the turn. This mini-challenge is also in David, who listens to Ana's turn and is not sure what she will say but wants to understand it to respond. Right after Ana finishes her turn, David then has the mini-challenge of responding clearly to what Ana just said, starting this mini-challenge process over again.

These quick and frequent real-time mini-challenges motivate students to engage more fully in the use of language because they feel the purpose in what they're doing: they are coming up with their own ideas and their own ways of understanding them rather than just memorizing them. Brains "on conversation" get lots of vital practice in the authentic uses of language—which is very different from the use of language that is motivated by getting points or simply displaying one's knowledge of words and rules.

Now picture a class of 30 students. Each student therefore has 29 different possible partners with whom to converse. This means repeated exposure to 29 different backgrounds, perspectives, and ways of using language to express and build ideas. And even if Student A in a pair is more proficient than Student B, Student A is challenged to clarify his or her ideas in each turn to Student B while also being challenged to understand new ideas presented by Student A. It's a win-win!

Let's say that, of these 30 students, several are learners at beginning levels of proficiency. These learners benefit from partnering with more proficient speakers who use lots of language to clarify their ideas. More proficient partners might use gestures, synonyms, drawings, and extra explanations to get their ideas across to less proficient speakers. Naturally, beginners will listen to more language than they produce, but this is a necessary stage, and having one-on-one partners and model language users on a frequent basis is highly effective. At the same time, teachers can and should provide students at beginning levels of proficiency with extra conversation scaffolding, such as graphic organizers, sentence starters, filling in needed background knowledge, and extra modeling of how to articulate disciplinary thinking and prompting within a conversation.

Giving Up and Taking Control

Conversations also push students to learn how to listen and value the ideas of others. On the surface, this means that students build habits of showing how much they value the ideas of others. We all know adults who have not built these habits—and it doesn't help them in life. On a deeper level, for some students this means learning to give up control and not being afraid to let others take the conversation in different directions. In doing so, students are pushed, in a good way, to pause their ongoing mental monologues and step outside of how they think about the world. They become, let's say, more human because their minds were made to grow and bloom when exposed to the ideas of others.

Still other students can learn to take more control as they engage in conversations with others. Many of these students have learned to "do school" without talking much at all. Some students get good grades; others are shy and don't want to make mistakes; others are bored. Through modeling, scaffolding, and practice, these students can learn to value their own ideas and share them—even with imperfect language—to contribute to effective conversations and to learning overall.

Paralinguistic Cues

Finally, another major benefit of conversation is learning how to communicate with paralinguistic cues. A lot of communication between two people involves body language, eye contact, and prosody, which includes stress and intonation. As students are immersed in conversations with others, they pick up ways of communicating from others. Similarly, they experiment with, prune, and reinforce their own extralinguistic strategies. In the class of 30 students, Student A gets to see how 29 other people use gestures and prosody to communicate. Students, over the years, learn not only the important paralinguistic cues used in mainstream academic and professional communications but also cues used by students of diverse backgrounds. Students can't develop these skills from books, and they can't show it on bubble-in tests. And yet these strategies can—and often do—make a big difference in the future (e.g., job interviews and relationships).

REFLECT AND APPLY

First off, think about how you can model and scaffold the skills of overcoming mini-challenges, giving up and taking control, and using paralinguistic clues. Try putting a student-student conversation up on the wall and revealing it line by line, acting it out with a student. Then point out the skills to students line by line, as suggested by the statements in the right-hand column of the following table. You can also point out other conversation skills. This sample conversation happens in fifth grade, prompted by the question of why it was called the Boston Massacre.

Conversation Transcript	What to Point Out to Students
Student: Why do you think the author wrote this?	*"Notice how my partner took control of the conversation with a question."*
Teacher: I think it was to describe what happened the night of what they call the Boston Massacre. But I don't think it was a massacre. Not enough people died. Only seven, I think. See what I mean?	*"Notice how I tried to overcome the mini-challenge of describing this new idea, an idea that challenges common knowledge of the event."*
Student: Yeah, I think so. You think they used *massacre* to make it sound worse?	*"Notice how my partner paraphrased and added information to overcome the mini-challenge of understanding the new idea introduced."*

Conversation Transcript	What to Point Out to Students
Teacher: Why would they do that?	*"Notice how I took control of the conversation with a question. I also used the paralinguistic cue of lifting up both hands to show questioning."*
Student: To make people mad, I think. For example. You would get mad if you hear about a massacre of your people, right? I would too. Probably madder than if just seven people died. Maybe it would get more people to fight.	*"Notice how my partner used* you *and herself as ways to overcome the mini-challenge of explaining her idea of getting people mad enough to fight. She used paralinguistic cues such as stressing certain words and physically pointing to me, and to herself, then to the text."*
Teacher: You mean to fight against the British?	*"Notice how I clarified to overcome the mini-challenge of understanding the previous idea. Notice also that I gave up control, allowing my partner to continue to explain her idea."*
Student: Yeah. They didn't all want to fight. I read that a lot of more . . . how do I say, comfortable people, people with good jobs, wanted things to stay the same.	*"Notice how this person works hard to explain the type of people who didn't want to fight."*
Teacher: It would be interesting to find out what percentage of people wanted to revolt and why. I wonder what I would have done back then. Would I want to fight a war?	*"Notice how I take control at the end, posing a question that requires clearer data than just 'not all of them.' I then personalize it a little to prompt some perspective taking on both our parts."*

CONVERSATION SKILLS

One of the ways in which we can help students make effective choices in their interactions with others is to develop several key conversation skills (Zwiers, O'Hara, & Pritchard, 2014). Unfortunately, many educators, students, and people walking down the street don't have a clear enough idea of what is involved in effective conversational discourse. Many students, for example, think that all conversations are arguments to win or that they involve just one person sharing an answer with another, as what happens in most

Think-Pair-Shares. The notion that you can respond back and forth with a partner to build up and negotiate ideas is rare in students.

An effective conversation in school has and does several things that we can see and hear. First, it changes something. This means that in the mind of participants, the information, ideas, or feelings about a topic are built up, strengthened, clarified, or changed in some way. For example, I might talk with a friend about the election coming up and learn his or her views on a certain candidate. I share my views, some of which clash with his or hers, and I see the characteristics that I value in a candidate more clearly than I did before our conversation. Second, a conversation has evidence of conversation skills. These skills, described in detail in this section, include clarifying ideas, supporting ideas with evidence and reasoning, evaluating evidence and reasoning, comparing the strength of ideas to choose the strongest one, and negotiating ideas.

In every conversation, there should be the building or changing of at least one idea. This usually requires a combination of both clarifying and supporting the idea with evidence and reasons. Then, if another competing idea pops up, it becomes an argument, and students then build up the second idea, too, also by clarifying and supporting it. After building up both (or all, if more than two) ideas, students evaluate the amount and quality of support on both sides to choose the "strongest" or "heaviest" one. Picture a balance scale with weights on both sides (see the conversation between Mayra and Ben that follows). If there is not a clear winner, then students can negotiate and qualify their ideas. This process of jointly and respectfully building up two or more ideas and choosing one is what we call *collaborative argumentation*. Students don't choose sides right away and "fight with words" to win; rather, they work together. Examples of both modes of conversation (building one idea and collaborative argumentation) are provided next.

The Skill of Clarifying Ideas

To get an effective conversation going, one student starts the conversation by responding to a prompt, posing a relevant idea to start talking about. This idea, in most cases, will not be clear to the listener the first time it's described. The listening partner will then prompt for clarification of this idea, asking something like "What do you mean by . . ." as you see Ilsa do in Line 3 of the following conversation.

(1) Ilsa: So, the teacher asked us why people are biased in history.

(2) Ana: I think they want to look good.

(3) Ilsa: What do you mean by that?

(4) Ana: They lie, like maybe leave out stuff so that they're like heroes or something.

(5) Ilsa: Yeah, like when the teacher said even us; we like don't say the whole truth when we tell our parents stuff.

(6) Ana: So, you're saying that we are like those people who lie in history?

(7) Ilsa: Yeah, kind of. Remember that guy, John Smith. He made up stuff, like on Pocahontas, to sell books.

(8) Ana: Can you say more about that? I read it but don't remember.

To clarify, a partner can do several things: ask for definitions (Line 3), ask for elaboration (Line 8), and paraphrase (Line 6). As you saw in the excerpt, clarifying can help to prompt a partner to produce more language, which (1) provides input for the listener and (2) challenges the speaker to put ideas into more and/or better words. This extra language used, as you see Ana produce in Line 4 and Ilsa produce in Line 7, helps both partners to think about the content being discussed. Complex ideas are more likely to "stick" because students are taking ownership of them—along with the language that describes them—to co-construct meaning together.

One challenge that we face is that students' communication experiences tend to be with people who know them well. They have not had to do much clarifying because family and peers tend to already know a lot about what they are saying. They have not needed to explain more complex, multi-sentence ideas very often to others for authentic purposes, so they don't develop habits of being extra explicit for a wider range of people.

Thus, one of the biggest needs for students developing academic language is a chance to practice their abilities to describe complex ideas to others and receive immediate feedback related to how clear it is. Conversations contain many turns, and many of these turns are attempts and opportunities to clarify. A partner listens and then offers nonverbal or verbal confirmation of clarity or lack thereof, giving feedback to the speaker to do something more or something different with language to get the idea across.

How clarifying within conversations fosters academic language and literacy

Imagine getting feedback on how clear you are from 29 or more different people on a weekly basis in multiple conversations with hundreds of turns in which you speak and listen. The effect on your literacy, language, knowledge, and thinking can be profound. Even if a highly proficient girl converses with a less proficient boy, both benefit from the process of seeking clarity. The highly proficient speaker is challenged to make her ideas extra clear, and the less proficient student benefits from extra language input—and from trying to make his ideas clear to her.

Students who are clarifying ideas about what they are reading can help one another with the content and language of complex texts. As students are encouraged to go back into texts to clarify what they are trying to get across, they refer to language in the text and use it in their turns.

The Skill of Supporting Ideas

Supporting ideas means using examples, evidence, and reasoning to logically ground or strengthen an idea. This is an essential skill for productive conversations in school, work, and life. Supporting ideas is necessary in most disciplines learned in school. In science, for example, students need to use observed data to support scientific conclusions. In math students must refer to mathematical principles to support a solution method they are using. In language arts, students need to use evidence from a story to support an idea for a theme. And in history students need to use evidence from primary sources to support a theory about the main causes or effects of an event.

Many students, and especially linguistically diverse students, need to overcome two challenges when it comes to supporting ideas. The first is finding the evidence in the first place. How, for example, do students learn to find evidence that supports a given theme in a novel? Some modeling and examples from teachers over the years, of course, helps to apprentice students in this skill. But talking with other students also provides exposure to a variety of evidence ideas as well as a variety of responses to one's own examples of evidence posed within a conversation. Over time, students form ideas for what is evidence and what is not.

The second challenge is effectively evaluating the value of evidence. A student might find nine examples that range in their support of how people viewed going to war. Students need to be able to weed out the weak examples and keep and highlight the strong evidence. Again, conversations can help. In fact, they have helped all of us. Through countless conversations in various settings with a variety of people, we have been exposed to a wide range of ideas, arguments, interpretations, and so on, many of which have been supported by what our conversation partners consider to be strong evidence and reasoning. We have posed our own ideas, supported them, and noticed how others have responded. The more often conversation partners don't value a certain type of evidence or reasoning, let's say referring to a family member to make a generalization about society, the more that we realize that this type of evidence might not be as strong as others.

See what happens in the conversation that follows, in which students look for a significant change in a main character in a story.

(1) Kara: So, Cassandra changes. She learns to respect old people.

(2) Leo: Can you give an example of that?

(3) Kara: I think when she helped her uncle find the kitten.

(4) Leo: OK. But she could help him and still not respect him, right? And he's not that old.

(5) Kara: You have one?

(6) Leo: Maybe when she reads her diary and dreams about it.

(7) Kara: How's that respect?

(8) Leo: It kinda shows that she thinks about her grandma, I guess. Like she starts to see how hard it was for her grandma to not give up. And she/

(9) Kara: /Here in the end of the book, she asked her mother, "Did Grandma do all that stuff she says during those dust storms? Did she do all those jobs for you and uncle?" And then she said, "Wow!" In the beginning of the story she was like, "I don't want to visit her. All she does is tell the same stories."

(10) Leo: That's a good example. Then she also goes to Grandma's house at the end to help her clean it and hear more stories.

How supporting ideas in conversation fosters academic language and literacy

Using this skill in conversation can help develop students' language in several ways. First, even before the conversation, it encourages students to look and relook through complex texts in search of valuable evidence. This provides a large amount of academic language input from texts. This input is then reinforced when a partner quotes or paraphrases the evidence from a text, as seen in Lines 3, 6, 8, and 9. To express support, a student needs to describe the example and, ideally, how it supports the idea, as seen in Lines 6 and 8. This pushes students to quickly and repeatedly put multiple sentences together for academic purposes. Supporting ideas involves very different thinking than just summarizing a text or recounting events in a story. It pushes students to use the information in a text in new ways that challenge complex thinking and uses of language.

This skill also helps students read and write more effectively. Being able to quickly identify evidence in a text while reading helps a reader construct the intended meaning of a text much more efficiently. As they develop their skill of weeding out and critiquing weaker evidence while, at the same time, identifying the strongest possible evidence to include in their conversations, this transfers over into writing.

The Skill of Evaluating Evidence and Reasoning

Different pieces of evidence often differ in how strongly they support an idea. Students need to be able to evaluate the strength, weight, and worth of multiple pieces of evidence and reasoning to decide whether and how to use it. But how does a student—or any human, for that matter—know if one piece of evidence is stronger, more valuable, or more reasonable than a different piece of evidence? Students must be apprenticed into what makes evidence valuable in a given discipline. As adults, we have had many conversations and experiences that have apprenticed us into knowing when evidence is weak or strong.

To evaluate evidence in academic settings, we tend to use criteria, which can vary across disciplines and contexts. For example, in the conversation that follows, students compare the criterion of frequency to the criterion of risking one's life. They decide that frequency weighs more in this case. Other criteria, commonly used in school and work settings, include financial costs and gains, health risks, number of people affected positively or negatively, human rights, short-term benefits, long-term benefits, ethical considerations, statistics, biases, and relevance, to name a few. As you can see by this short list, one of the greatest gifts we can give students is the capacity to work with others in using criteria to evaluate evidence.

The "quantity-focused" approach to learning, described in Chapter 1, can negatively influence the skill of gathering evidence. For many students, finding three examples to use as evidence means finding the first three that come along. They are answers, or blanks to fill in, in a sense. Instead, we must foster the mind-set of seeking to communicate as strongly and clearly as possible, which requires finding the highest-quality evidence, even if it means— perish the thought—more rereading to build the strongest possible argument or idea.

One type of evidence evaluation is ranking the strengths of evidences that support one idea. This is needed when a person must decide which evidence best supports a position. In a classroom conversation we can encourage students to share how much they value pieces of evidence and why—the why is based on criteria. In the following conversation, for example, the teacher prompts students to evaluate multiple pieces of evidence for Sacagawea being a hero.

(1) Paty: I think cuz she help others on the trip, not selfish.

(2) Leah: Like how?

(3) Paty: Food. They need it and warm clothes. She show them how to get them.

(4) Leah: Like when she went at night and got roots that they could eat? And the bear. She risked her life to save Clark. That's a hero.

(5) Paty: And she was calm when Chief Green Cat came. That's hero, when you are scared and you stay calm. Maybe it saved them not to be killed, and/

(6) Leah: /And they're different than her, but she's still nice to them.

(7) Paty: But what's the strongest?

(8) Leah: I think the bear one.

(9) Paty: Why?

(10) Leah: Cuz she risked her life.

(11) Paty: I think being nice and helping them, a pesar de (despite) they are white. The bear was just one time, but she's nice every day, like she find roots to eat.

(12) Leah: I can agree with that. But I like the bear story.

The second type of evaluation of evidence happens in collaborative argumentation. A *collaborative argument* is one in which students work together to build up each side of an issue and then objectively evaluate the total "weight" or "strength" on each side to choose the heavier or stronger one. Students still might evaluate one piece of evidence on a side to clarify its strength or weight, but the overall goal in this second type of evaluation is to see which side weighs more. Here is an example from an eighth-grade history class. Both students are academic ELLs.

(1) Mayra: One side is industrialization was bad.

(2) Ben: What do you mean, bad?

(3) Mayra: For example, there's crime and dangerous. You saw the pictures. Right?

(4) Ben: Yeah, lots of sick people. And the article said it hurt people a lot. I think/

(5) Mayra: I think people got sick, and some did crime cuz machines take their jobs.

(6) Ben: And lots of pollution.

(7) Mayra: Like how did industrialization make pollution more bad?

(8) Ben: The factories dumped it into rivers, and they/

(9) Mayra: /And lots of smoke in the air.

(10) Ben: Yeah, so what about the good side of it?

(11) Mayra: It helped people buy cheaper things.

(12) Ben: How?

(13) Mayra: The factories made lots of things in one day, so they cost less, for example, cars.

(14) Ben: And people got jobs in factories, so they got to work and get paid.

(15) Mayra: And they could have better lives at home with inventions made in factories.

(16) Ben: OK, so which side is stronger or heavier?

(17) Mayra: I dunno. Like the job thing is on both sides.

(18) Mayra: Some people lost jobs, and some people got jobs. I don't know what was better.

(19) Ben: Yeah, so maybe they are even. But the pollution got way worse.

(20) Mayra: Yeah. But does pollution weigh more than some of the inventions that made life easier?

(21) Ben: I think so. Pollution kills animals and makes people sick.

(22) Mayra: I agree, but factories also make medicines, and they also/

(23) Ben: /They make bombs, too!

(24) Mayra: OK, so let's say it is more on the bad side.

(25) Ben: OK.

This conversation was supported by the Argument Balance Scale, a visual scaffold described at the end of this chapter. Notice how Ben and Mayra built one idea and then built the opposing idea. Neither student started with an obvious choice of side or desire to "win" the argument. They both contributed to both ideas, and evidence emerged that they both could use in the later evaluation and choice they made. They compared two similar pieces of evidence, jobs lost and created, and then decided that factories making bombs as well as causing sickness and death caused the "bad" side to weigh more. Notice that there was a lot of critical thinking and lots of real language used.

Why did this conversation sound different than typical competitive arguments? The students resisted three major temptations. The first temptation is shutting the other student down and not allowing him or her to build ideas that contradict yours. The second temptation is not sharing evidence or clarifications that would help to build a side that contradicts yours. The third temptation is being unwilling to change your mind based on the conversation and the evidence presented on both sides. As a teacher, you can watch for students giving in to these temptations and intervene with mini-lessons and modeling when needed.

How evaluating evidence and reasoning in conversations fosters academic language and literacy

With few exceptions, each person in the world has a different idea of exactly how much value a piece of evidence has in supporting a claim. Student A thinks the statistics in an article on global warming are very supportive and valuable, whereas Student B does not. They both need to explain why. And when students have varying ideas and opinions, especially about abstract things like the value of evidence or the quality of reasoning, then rich language is needed.

The industrialization conversation also highlights an important thinking skill that students need to learn: weighing apples and oranges. This means comparing and evaluating two very unlike sides, types of evidence, or criteria. In Line 20, Mayra asks, "But does pollution weigh more than some of the inventions that made life easier?" The students, in the end, agreed quickly, but this question is a very real question, even today. Life is full of decisions between apples and oranges, and students need a heavy amount of exposure to them within a variety of topics. In conversations like this one, students can collaborate and productively struggle to figure out how they will most clearly and most effectively evaluate evidence to choose a side. And in most cases, we don't care which side they choose, as long as their minds are exhausted from thinking and describing it with their ever-developing academic discourse.

Negotiating Ideas

As people in a conversation attempt to decide which idea has stronger or heavier evidence, often there isn't a clear winner. "It's not a black-and-white situation" is a common expression in the real world. Often there are conditions that need to be described and applied to clarify, qualify, or validate the winning side of an issue. This is negotiation, which involves making concessions and agreeing to choose a side under certain conditions. In fact, in many "apples-and-oranges" situations, there is a need to negotiate meanings.

Let's take a quick look at an example of negotiation. A group of three students are nearing the end of a conversation on whether or not to use the DNA of extinct species of animals and plants to bring them back out of extinction.

(1) Tania: Yeah, I think yes, but the species should be safe in scientific laboratories. They shouldn't be out in the wild cuz who knows what will happen.

(2) Alex: I think they will get out, or some disease might get out, like in the movies. So I agree, but only, like the condition they bring back species that were extinct because of us. We caused it, so we should fix it.

(3) Hector: It might be too late to fix. In the video it said that some ecosystems are already adjusted. Putting an animal back in could mess it up. So I am mostly no, unless it can help us solve big health problems like cancer.

(4) Tania: OK, so what if we say that we bring species back that we killed off? We keep them in labs and try to solve health problems with them. But we don't hurt them.

Notice that all of the students were in favor at some level but had different conditions and different ways of describing their ideas.

They negotiated their ideas, and Tania, in Line 4, did a final negotiation of the three ideas in Lines 1 through 3.

How negotiating in conversations fosters academic language and literacy

Negotiating adds another language-rich layer to conversation. Notice the language that students used: *with the condition*; *should be contained*; *not be reintroduced*; *unknowns*; and *unless*. Students need to use—and listen to—advanced language like this to describe the strong and weak points in their own and opposing arguments and to explain their reasoning to come up with a logical position that they can defend. Negotiating requires students to think about the value of abstract ideas on each side of an issue, not just quickly choose a side, as if it were an answer on a multiple choice test. Negotiating also allows students to personalize their ideas even more, which fosters more ownership of complex language.

Competitive Argumentation

A more common type of argument in school (and in the real world) is competitive, one in which students pick a side and try to win. Even though they often spark quite a bit of energy and talk, if not properly facilitated, their side effects can limit the participation of many students, particularly those who need the most practice talking. Often, dominant students, wanting to win at all costs, won't even let others have the floor or share the evidence for the opposing sides. True, there are effective classroom activities that are competitive, such as debates, Socratic seminars, and philosophical chairs. We should continue to use these. But students must also learn how to collaborate and be objective when deciding between ideas or choosing sides of an issue.

REFLECT AND APPLY

1. Why do you think students (and adults) tend to lack these conversation skills?

2. Listen to a conversation between two people you know (or your students), and listen for these skills.

CREATE A CLASSROOM CULTURE
OF COLLABORATIVE COMMUNICATION

Productive conversational discourse is, on average, rare in most classrooms, especially in schools that serve diverse students. Why? A major reason is that teachers and students, traditionally, have not considered it to be useful for classroom learning. Many teachers have not known of the many benefits of building students' conversation skills and using conversations to teach. Another reason is that educators have typically not had high expectations for what students can do in conversations.

Another reason is that we haven't been testing collaboration with high-stakes assessments. These assessments, largely multiple-choice in nature and focused on choosing right answers related to reading and math tasks, have significantly shaped teaching practices—especially in schools with low scores. Conversational discourse, which involves shaping and negotiating complex ideas, doesn't fit into a short, right-answer-focused curriculum and testing system.

To create a productive collaborative classroom culture, several shifts must happen. First, we must fortify our belief that students can work together to build ideas, manage their interactions, and make logical decisions as they cultivate their disciplinary thinking and communication skills. The focus of learning needs to shift from simply knowing the facts to using them as raw material to build understandings with them. We need to shift to placing much higher priority on communicating ideas and concepts with a wide range of others. We should want students to be thinking, "I really want to understand this idea to clearly communicate it to others" rather than "I really want to memorize this idea to get it right on a test for points." This shift entails moving from individual knowing and thinking to working, thinking, and knowing together—which means spending more time in conversation than ever before in our classrooms.

Conditions for Fostering Conversational Discourse

Conversation-based learning requires several conditions that allow productive interactions within and across lessons to thrive. The first condition is a safe space for students to share their ideas without being mocked or laughed at. Students need to feel that they can share any idea that they think is valuable, even if it contradicts the majority. This condition is obvious and easy enough on paper, but kids can be mean at any time, so we must be ever vigilant in maintaining this condition.

The second condition is the valuing of conversation as a way to learn. Many students (and teachers) view learning as mainly coming from books or teacher lectures. They don't see the value of building ideas with others, articulating their own developing ideas, and listening to perspectives of peers.

The third condition is the curriculum itself. Is the curriculum set up in such a way that conversations are helpful or needed to accomplish tasks that foster learning? Are the questions in the curriculum appropriate for conversations? Do conversations contribute to eventual success on performance tasks and other assessments? For example, a teacher might prompt students to come up with a poster presentation for younger students that explains the phases of the moon. First, students converse about their hypotheses, then they read a text and watch a video, and finally they converse about how to best represent the key ideas in a poster. All along, the teacher uses conversations strategically to strengthen content concepts, thinking skills, and language.

Features of Communicativeness

Communicativeness is the amount and quality of communication that happens between students. For communicativeness to be present, conversations need to have useful and engaging purposes for them. We can't just say, "Talk about this chapter for several minutes" and expect much energy put into conversing. Students need to know why they are talking to others to muster up the energy that it takes to effectively converse with others. So, the first feature is having an engaging purpose for conversing with another person.

The prompt usually makes a big difference in the quality of conversations. A prompt for any conversation should have clear enough purpose that involves sharing and building ideas in support of the objectives of the lesson. A prompt should also require academic thinking and reshaping, choosing, or doing something with ideas. Here are some samples of verbs that you can use in prompts: *agree on, create, clarify, argue, decide, rank, prioritize, come up with, solve, evaluate, combine, compare, choose, fortify, build, weigh,* and *transform.* Here are some examples of decent prompts:

- Decide which theme in the story is most relevant for fourth graders today.
- Come to an agreement on how you would measure the speed of sound.
- Discuss how to solve this problem two different ways, and argue for the use of one of them in future problems that are similar.
- Rank the qualities of a good friend.
- For our museum project, work with a partner to decide on the clearest way to describe the importance of each artifact and what it tells us about people in that time period.

When students think that a conversation is just another pair-share to say an answer and listen to a partner's answer, conversation doesn't happen. We want them to be excited by the prompt and by the chance to think together with others about it. Students need to see conversations as vital stages leading toward the completion of larger engaging tasks.

High-quality communicativeness also depends on information gaps, which is the second feature. This means that students have ideas to share that are not already known by partners. If students read different texts, for example, they are more likely to have ideas from the texts—as well as their own interpretations of the text—to share with others in conversation. Students work a lot harder to put ideas into language if those ideas are not already known by others. Also, the brain gets authentic practice in its use of language—which is very different from the use of language that is motivated by points or simply displaying one's knowledge of words and rules.

If the students we are concerned about had a lot more time in school to adequately build the wide range of language knowledge and skills needed for the future, then the first two features would be enough. But for many diverse students and ELLs, the short class periods and noninteractive lessons in school are not enough. So, a third feature of communicativeness is attention to language. This means that before, during, and after conversations in a lesson, there is extra teaching and assessment focused on improving how language is used to effectively converse. This includes structuring talking situations, modeling, practicing, giving feedback, and/or scaffolding. It might even include the strategic development of grammar or vocabulary that helps students to communicate. Based on what we observe that students need, we model and scaffold whatever aspects of language that we want to emphasize to help students communicate.

REFLECT AND APPLY

Use the section you just read and other resources to create a tool for creating and measuring the quality of collaboration mindedness in your classroom. Prioritize the value of the features and what is most needed by your students.

SCAFFOLDS FOR CONVERSATION SKILLS

Obviously, you can't just assign a reading or give a lecture on effective conversation skills and expect stellar conversations the next day. It takes a lot of time, modeling, scaffolding, and varied practice to build these skills for use with a wide range of topics and conversation partners. Fortunately, there are several scaffolds that we can use.

Conversation Skills Poster

The first scaffold is a pair of posters with the main conversation skills and icons that symbolize them. (See Figure 3.1.) The posters can be used during conversations to remind students of skills, to keep them focused on focal ideas, and to help them keep going when the conversation stalls (Zwiers et al., 2014). As you explain and model each skill, you can reinforce it with hand motions, which we will describe in parentheses.

You can start with the "Build 1 Idea" mode. In the center is the initial idea that partners are trying to build. This serves as a reminder to stay focused. Someone needs to first create or pose a potentially valuable idea (hand motion: put wrists together down low, and move hands up and outward, like a tree growing). Then they work to clarify the idea (make binoculars from both hands, and put up to eyes) and support it with examples, evidence, and reasons (put out one hand palm down; put other hand out underneath with five fingers pointed up, supporting the other hand).

Now, for the second poster, which represents the "Build > 1 Idea and Choose" mode, this is conversation about choosing the strongest of two or more sides of an argument. When a second idea that competes with the first emerges, students build it up, too, bringing up evidence as well as its strengths and weaknesses. Then students compare the evidence weight on each side and choose the heaviest side (hand motion: put both arms out to the side, palms up, and move up and down like a balance scale). Teachers have adapted and used this poster in a variety of ways. Feel free to experiment.

Figure 3.1 Conversation Skills Posters

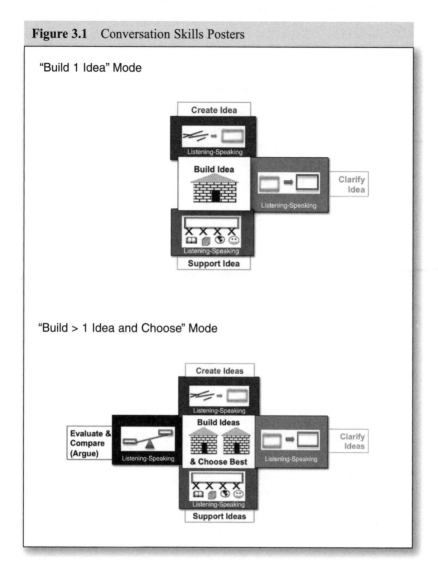

If-When Chart

You can use and adapt the If-When chart to help students when they get stuck. The "You" at the top of the second column refers to the student, not the teacher, although teachers can benefit from this chart, too, in conversations with students. If or when students have problems in a conversation, they can refer to the chart to help them move along. You can also listen and refer students to certain rows if appropriate.

If . . . or When . . .	You Can . . .
1. The conversation doesn't start well or at all,	• Say, "Let's understand (clarify or define) this. . . What we need to do is . . ." • Ask, "What does . . . mean in this case (context or situation)? • Say, "Let's scan through the text again and look for . . ." • Say, "Let's take two different sides; which one do you want?
2. Your partner offers a short response,	• Ask for specific clarification or elaboration. • Ask a question (Why? How? I wonder why/how. . .). • Ask what a word or expression means. • Ask for an example that supports it. • Give an example, and ask if your partner agrees.
3. Your partner offers a long and confusing response,	• Paraphrase it, and relate it to the conversation purpose. • Ask to clarify the most relevant part of the response. • Ask for additional evidence or examples.
4. Your partner shares a piece of evidence,	• Ask how the evidence supports the idea. • Add your own explanation for how well it supports the idea. • Ask how well the evidence supports the idea. • Ask for additional evidence and examples: "What is other evidence that might support your idea?" • Compare and contrast it to other evidence.
5. Share your idea, and get little response ("Yeah, OK, uh huh, or hmmm),	• Ask your partner what he or she thinks about your idea. • Ask your partner for his or her evidence for your idea. • Tell your partner to disagree with you, so you can make your idea stronger. • Ask, "Do we have enough evidence to argue this idea?"

If-When Chart for What to Say Next (from Zwiers et al., 2014).

For example, fourth-grade teacher, Ms. Nguyen, noticed that some students were responding to their partners' ideas about animal adaptations with short responses such as "I agree" and "OK." She tells students to use some of the ideas in Rows 2 and 5 of the chart, which are on the board in the front of the room. She then works with one pair of students, who have the following conversation:

(1) Lisa: I think animals change to help them live and not die from other animals.

(2) Bryan: I agree. They change a lot. (The conversation stalls.)

The teacher suggests to both of them to think about what they might say next to deepen or extend the conversation. Bryan looks at the If-When chart and says, "From Row 2 I could say, 'Why do you think animals change? What are examples?' or I could even argue with her, just to make it fun. I could say that horses have been horses for a long time." Lisa says, "And I could say, 'How do they change? And why do you think they change?'" Ms. Nguyen, before moving to another pair, encourages them to use these moves to keep building ideas in the conversation.

Observer Cards

Observer cards allow an observer (teacher or peer) to support a conversation without getting verbally involved. One of the biggest problems, especially with teacher observations, is that the teacher becomes the dominant third wheel in a conversation. Instead, the teacher (or peer observer) can use cards that have various prompts on them. The observer (teacher or student) can put the card in front of either partner or out in the middle when appropriate. This should happen when it is clear that they need help: they are not talking, they are off topic, they are arguing un-academically, and so on. They can also be color coded: purple for cards that prompt for the creating of ideas; red for clarifying; blue for supporting; and green for evaluating and comparing. The prompts can be images, words, or sentence frames. Here are some observer card ideas:

Ask for an (another) example to support the idea	Paraphrase what your partner said	Ask your partner to clarify (Why . . . How . . . Define the term)
Show that you are listening with your eyes, nods, and posture	Pose a competing idea and start to build it up	Refer to the conversation prompt
Encourage your partner to talk more	Summarize the conversation up until now	Ask for criteria used to evaluate evidence

Observer Card Ideas (from Zwiers et al., 2014)

The following example of a conversation in a fifth-grade math classroom was prompted by a question: "When dividing fractions, why do we multiply by the reciprocal of one of the fractions?" Notice at which points the teacher decides to pass cards to students, and consider why.

(1) Kara: I think cuz divide is the opposite of multiply.

(2) Tran: So why don't we turn both fractions over and multiply?

(3) Kara: I don't know. (Conversation stalls.)

(4) *Teacher:*   *(Passes the **Define the term** card to Kara.)*

(5) Kara: What does divide mean?

(6) Tran: To see how many times it fits.

(7) Kara: What do you mean?

(8) Tran: I don't know. You see how many times it fits!

(9) *Teacher:*   *(Passes the **Ask for an example** card to Kara.)*

(10) Kara: Can you give an example?

(11) Tran: Like an example six divided by two. Two fits in six three times.

(12) Kara: Yeah, that's easy, but how do we see how many times fractions fit? Like this one, 2/3 divided by 3/10. It's too hard to draw, so we just do the reciprocal thing.

(13) Tran: Yeah, I agree. (Conversation stalls.)

(14) *Teacher:*   *(Passes the **Refer to the conversation prompt** card to Tran.)*

(15) Tran: But why do we do the reciprocal?

(16) Kara: OK, so for six divided by two, here, if you can put one over two and multiply it to six. You get six times a half, and that's three, right?

(17) Tran: But how you know to put the one over it?

(18) Kara: I don't know. But when you divide numbers, I think you can also multiply by one over it, and that's a fraction. So it should work with fractions, too, right?

Notice how the teacher chose certain stalled and weak spots in the conversation to insert the cards without adding his or her own voice to the mix. The cards helped her help students become more independent in their conversation moves.

Students can watch you model how to observe and support conversations with the cards like the ones here. They can also become conversation coaches who observe conversations, use the cards, and reflect on other students' conversations so that they can do well in their own. Some teachers simply have triads rotate roles (Student A, Student B, and observer) over the course of a unit. Some teachers have pairs use several cards without coaches. Students can refer to the cards and even "play" them as they converse.

Use Whole-Class Discussions to Develop Conversational Discourse

Even with their limitations, you can use whole-class discussions to model and scaffold the most effective moves for building ideas with others. When a student poses an initial idea, you can model and prompt students to clarify, support, and evaluate. For example, when a sixth-grade student said, "I think the Qin Shi Huang was an effective leader," the teacher responded, "Interesting idea. What might you say to get Lorena to clarify or strengthen her idea?" Students said, "Why do you think that? What evidence could support your idea? What do you mean by effective?"

Some other whole-class discussion ideas include coming up with gestures to fortify discussion and develop the skills. Students show one finger to share a way to clarify, support, or add to a current idea; two fingers to challenge the idea; and three fingers to share a new or opposing idea. The teacher uses one- and two-finger responses before moving on to the three-fingered new ideas. Or a teacher can also raise his or her own finger, which signals students to ask others to clarify or support the idea, and so on.

Written Conversations

Another way to both see and develop students' conversational discourse skills is to work with a partner to write a conversation down on paper or a computer. This takes more time than actual talking, but it gives them a different view of how a conversation forms and a bit more time to consider what they can do to strengthen it.

It also allows you, the teacher, to gather their papers or digital versions to see what all students are saying and thinking, as opposed to just the few students you listen to during oral conversations. It also helps you and your students see a variety of conversation and language skills, such as connecting sentences within a turn. One student said, "Wow, I didn't realize that a conversation could be good or bad. I thought we just talked." You can also use some of these conversations as models up front to point out certain skills, language, and content understandings.

Whole-Class Analysis and Construction of Conversation Models

Teachers can use video or put up developing conversations up front, stop them, and ask students what a partner should say next before revealing what the student actually said. You can also create a developing conversation up front and write in what students think the participants should say at each turn for a great conversation to happen. You can put up good and bad models and discuss why they are good and bad. You can also have students use the If-When chart. These activities will help students to bulk up their awareness of conversation skills and how they work to accomplish purposes in conversations. The next section describes conversation skills in more detail.

Sentence Frames

Sentence frames can be good and bad. They can, when used strategically, sparingly, and optionally, help develop students' academic language as they use language to communicate. They can also hamper, hinder, and halt the flow of conversations as students look at a paper or the wall for the "right way to say" what they want to say. At best, they are minor and temporary supports for helping students communicate more clearly with language that is more academic than what tends to result in normal speech. Just remember that sentence frames are not enough. We must create rich contexts in which students want to have meaty conversations and need to clarify, support, negotiate, think critically, and so on. Most of the time, language development will come from the many messy back-and-forth turns in which students listen and speak to co-construct meaningful ideas over time.

Collaborative Argument Balance Scale

A helpful visual scaffold that supports and shows the skills of supporting and evaluating ideas is a conversation argument scale (Zwiers et al., 2014). (See Figure 3.2.) In pairs, students work together to build both sides and then converse about which side is stronger or "heavier" in terms of evidence and how well it supports the positions. As students discuss their differing ideas on how to evaluate and compare evidence on each side, lots of rich language is needed. For example, they need to use criteria, such as long- and short-term benefits and drawbacks, to make a decision and argue why they made it. You saw this type of conversation already between Ben and Mayra, who decided the Industrial Revolution was more negative than positive.

Figure 3.2   Collaborative Argument Balance Scale Visual Organizer

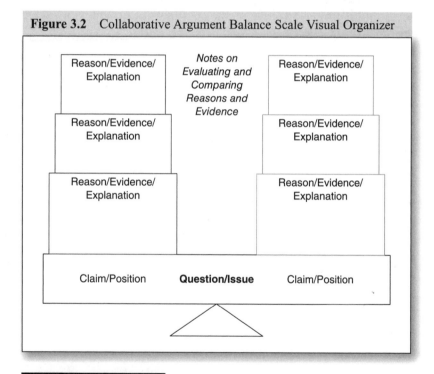

REFLECT AND APPLY

How might you adapt one or more of the scaffolds described in this chapter to meet your students' needs? Think of how it can be used in an upcoming lesson. Consider which scaffolds might work across disciplines.

CONCLUSION

It can be tempting to focus on the more visible effects of conversation, even those that show students' language and literacy abilities. But we must also think about the discourse skills themselves, the abilities to communicate, and capacities to connect with other humans. Conversations do more than teach content; they build students' abilities to get along with others, to respect diverse ideas, to listen, to ask questions, and to collaboratively solve problems. Conversations can also build a student's sense of academic identity and self-efficacy. When a student immerses him- or herself in rich conversations and contributes to the creation of a new idea, he or she helps to develop connections and understandings that weren't possible on his or her own. He or she sees him- or herself as a valued member of the class, school, and even the world.

CHAPTER FOUR

Learning From Classroom Examples of Conversational Discourse

In true conversation, the sparks fly as two ideas meet for the first time.

There is a vast range of conversations that can and do happen in K–12 classrooms. Just think of the difference between a first-grade conversation about a character in a story, a fifth-grade conversation about why gravity is different on the moon than on Earth, and a tenth-grade conversation about the main effects of World War I. Even in the same room at the same moment, students can have a wide variety of conversations about the same topic. So in the examples that follow, keep this in mind. They are not meant to be perfect models. Rather, they are meant to show you what is both common and possible with respect to conversational discourse in classroom settings. They are intended to spark reflection and insights that influence your own work with your students.

FIRST-GRADE LANGUAGE ARTS

First graders can have better conversations than you might think at first. With enough modeling and scaffolding (but not too much), they can use all of the skills of building ideas and arguing, even if they don't use the more advanced vocabulary and grammar of later grades. Indeed, the goal of conversation work in early years is more to establish a solid foundation and framework of social and conversation skills upon which students can "hang" increasingly academic language in the years to come. These skills include turn taking, eye contact, gestures, and intonation in addition to the skills of creating, clarifying, supporting, evaluating, and negotiating ideas.

In the following example, the teacher has read *The Little Red Hen* (Galdone, 2001) aloud to students. It is the story about a hen that works to prepare bread. The hen asks other animals to help in the preparation, and they decline. When they want to eat the bread, she doesn't share it with them. The teacher then prompts students to decide whether or not the little red hen should have shared her bread with the animals or not.

(1) Ana: I think she not share it (bread).

(2) Brian: Why?

(3) Ana: Cuz the other animals not work; just lazy.

(4) Brian: Yeah. I don't think to share, too.

(5) Ana: Why?

(6) Brian: Like my dad. He work for money. Not work, no money.

(7) Ana: Yeah, no es justo. They should/

(8) Brian: /Not fair. But teacher said is good to share.

(9) Ana: I share when they help. Like if I paint the school. I don't want others to get my money.

(10) Brian: No. Maybe if . . . no pueden . . . work, like they're sick, maybe. But the animals are lazy.

(11) Ana: Is good to share, but not all the time; not with lazies.

Notice that these two students co-construct an idea that was stronger than what either of them had in mind before the conversation. This is important. Something must change in a conversation: an idea gets stronger, an opinion shifts a bit, a concept is clarified, and so on. Also, we are looking for evidence of conversation skills. In Line 1 Ana creates the initial idea. In Lines 2 and 5 they each ask for clarification with "Why?". In Line 3 Ana supports her idea with evidence from the text; in Line 6 Brian supports the idea with an idea from his own life. In Line 8 Brian brings up an opposing idea that reenergizes the conversation and prompts both of them to come up with even more examples in support of the idea in Lines 9 and 10. And finally in Line 11 Ana does a nice job of synthesizing what they talked about into a final concluding idea.

SECOND-GRADE MATH

In the initial stage of the lesson, the teacher provides a launch problem and provides time for students to work on the problem and verbalize their understandings, questions, and ideas to others. Students explore and experiment with ways to solve the problem and then give reasons for doing so. The teacher reminds students to give good reasons for what they think they should do and to ask for reasons if a partner doesn't give them right away. As students talk, the teacher listens in for strong responses and misconceptions. She also supports students in using multiple and connected sentences together to create logical ideas.

(1) Teacher: OK, today in your conversations I want you to ask your partner what he or she is thinking and why he or she is doing something with the problem. Before you write anything, talk about what happens in the problem and what it is asking. I also want you to estimate the final answer and say why. You can start with "I think the answer will be . . . because . . ." And if your partner doesn't give a reason, ask why. Here is the problem: *Diana was out hiking and filled a plastic bag with blackberries. She gave five berries to her dog and eight to her friend Sofia. She had 12 left for her own lunch. How many berries did she have in her bag before giving some away?* Now pair up.

(2) Karla: I think she had more than 12.

(3) Miguel: Why?

(4) Karla: Cuz she gave some away and had 12 left.

(5) Miguel: I think like 30 cuz she gave some away and still had a lot. OK, how?

(6) Karla: Let's draw them. Here's a bag of berries.

(7) Miguel: How many?

(8) Karla: Lots. Maybe 30, like you said.

(9) Miguel: Then what?

(10) Karla: She gives 'em away. So, erase like five.

(11) Miguel: Why erase?

(12) Karla: Cuz they're gone. Now erase eight more. . . . Now count them.

(13) Miguel: Seventeen. That's not 12.

(14) Karla: I know it's not 12.

(15) Miguel: So what do we do?

(16) Karla: We started with too many. She needs to have 12 left, not 17.

(17) Miguel: So let's change it to 17. We can/

(18) Karla: /You mean change the problem? (Miguel nods his head.) We can't do that. We just need to get the answer.

(19) Miguel: OK, so we got too many. It's (counting on fingers) four, no five, too many, right? We can start with five less this time. So not 30, but 29, 28, 27, 26, 25.

(20) Karla: So, 25 berries. So to check it, we erase five, then eight; then it should be 12 left, right?

(21) Miguel: It is!

(22) Teacher: Nice work! Now what about a non-drawing way to solve it, using math like we have done this past week?

(23) Miguel: We use plus and minus and numbers and empty boxes.

(24) Karla: OK. We don't know how much in the bag, so a empty box for that.

(25) Miguel: And we draw a dog and her friend, and maybe we draw/

(26) Karla: /No, just numbers; we're not drawing this time.

(27) Miguel: We can put the box and minus five cuz she gives them to her dog.

(28) Karla: But my dog hates berries.

(29) Miguel: So what? It's still five less, so we minus five then minus eight cuz she gives eight to her friend, right?

(30) Karla: So empty box minus five minus eight equals 12, I guess.

(31) Miguel: How do we take five away from the box?

(32) Karla: I don't know. But we need a big number to start with.

(33) Miguel: We could just add what we got up and see.

(34) Karla: OK. It's . . . 25! We got the same number when we did the pictures.

The first thing that we notice here is the length of the conversation. The students keep going without much need for support, and they both contribute more or less equal amounts. The teacher only intervenes once in Line 22 to remind them to think of a second method for solving the problem. There is a large amount of language input and output for their brains to process. They are engaged in the math as they build ideas together. They challenge one another to think and clarify their thoughts, and they frequently prompt one another to explain reasons for doing things.

THIRD-GRADE SCIENCE

In this lesson students are learning how the moon doesn't change its actual shape from night to night, but rather, we only see differing portions of the moon's lit side. The eventual task that students need to perform is the presentation of a model of how and why the moon appears to change shape during the course of a month. Students had seen a short video explaining that the different angles at which the sun hits the moon on different nights accounts for its apparent change in shape over time. The conversation sample here is a discussion by two students on how to best communicate this phenomenon to others. Nia is considered to be an SEL, and Tarik is an L with intermediate levels of speaking and listening proficiency. Look for clarifying moves as well as for the beginnings of using academic language in science.

(1) Tarik: I don't get it.

(2) Nia: Get what?

(3) Tarik: Why shape changes.

(4) Nia: It doesn't change shape. Just looks like it cuz of light.

(5) Tarik: Orbit, moon.

(6) Nia: What about it?

(7) Tarik: Not same every night.

(8) Nia: Look at these balls. The light is the sun. This ball is us. The white ball is the moon.

(9) Tarik: They go 'round and/

(10) Nia: /Yeah, but we need to explain it.

(11) Tarik: Like why it change shape?

(12) Nia: It doesn't change shape. Just looks like it. It's round, like, always.

(13) Tarik: I know. But light is different from sun. We can draw it.

(14) Nia: OK. Make Earth. Put us here.

(15) Tarik: Why?

(16) Nia: Cuz you gotta be somewhere to see it, right?

(17) Tarik: Yeah. Now the moon on, like this, a orbit. Make arrows in circle. It moves and/

(18) Nia: /Put the sun over here. And make black the part of the moon where it's not all lighted.

(19) Tarik: But we gotta draw the moon in other places.

(20) Nia: Why?

(21) Tarik: Show changes. On one paper.

(22) Nia: OK. But it looks like we got four moons now. We can't/

(23) Tarik: /No. We just put time on it. Like Week 1, Week 2. And we say only one moon.

(24) Nia: So moons here and here and here. So when it's in the middle of us and the sun, we just see it dark, right?

(25) Tarik: We don't see it. But other side of Earth/

(26) Nia: /But on the other side of Earth, you see the whole thing. Full moon.

(27) Tarik: OK. And the side, here, we see part of light part of moon.

Notice how the purpose of clarifying and constructing a model that explains a complex phenomenon can foster a lot of rich language. In several turns the students prompted for clarification, such as in Lines 1, 3, 6, 10, 15, and 20. Clarifying is powerful because it helps the person asking for clarification to learn the concept better while also being exposed to more language. Tarik, especially, benefitted from this conversation in that he likely began the interaction with the misconception that the moon changed its actual shape. Nia helped to clarify this, and then Tarik actually helped her to see an effective way to model the phenomenon by drawing four moons on the poster.

FOURTH-GRADE HISTORY

Students are studying the California Gold Rush and were asked to discuss and decide on the best route to get to California from the New York. They chose from three routes: overland, around Cape Horn, and through the isthmus of Panama. Students knew the pros and cons of each route and now had to converse about them, evaluate them, and make a choice with a partner. The focal skill was evaluating evidence and explaining its value to others. Look for this skill and its language as well as other strengths and areas to improve. They used the Argument Balance Scale as a scaffold for their ideas. They put the positive reasons and evidence in the boxes and the negative reasons at the arrows that push the side up.

(1)	Noe:	So we gotta start with two of three.
(2)	Rahel:	I think the land and the Panama ones.
(3)	Noe:	Why?
(4)	Rahel:	Cuz for Cape Horn it was long, and you can't take family/
(5)	Noe:	/And it was dangerous. You can crash, like get wrecked, by waves and storms.
(6)	Rahel:	OK, this side is overland, and this side is Panama. We need evidence.
(7)	Noe:	Over land you can take family.
(8)	Rahel:	And you don't worry about storms or falling off the ship.
(9)	Noe:	But you get attacked, snakes get you, and . . . I don't know if/
(10)	Rahel:	/Winter you get cold and die. So the bad things go on arrows, right?
(11)	Noe:	Yeah. (They write.) And the other side?
(12)	Rahel:	The Panama route.
(13)	Noe:	It's fastest and same price like the route down around here.
(14)	Rahel:	That's in two boxes.
(15)	Noe:	But you can die from diseases.
(16)	Rahel:	Which ones?
(17)	Noe:	(Looks at book) Here. Malaria, cholera, yellow fever. Maybe/

(18) Rahel: /So they go on the arrows. To push it up.

(19) Noe: And also bad is storms and wreck the ship.

(20) Rahel: What is most heavy?

(21) Noe: I think over the land.

(22) Rahel: Why?

(23) Noe: Diseases kill you. Snakes not so bad. And cold don't kill you if you got coats and fire.

(24) Rahel: I think Panama is good. Is faster so not so much time out to get sick. Not so cold. No mountains or snow. And is most popular. What should we choose?

(25) Noe: I can change to Panama. I don't wanna push wagons over mountains.

(26) Rahel: Me too. OK, so we choose it. Cuz is warm, no snow, and is faster.

(27) Noe: OK.

Notice the collaborative argumentation in this conversation. They build the first idea (overland route) and then the second one (Panama isthmus route). After they have clarified and supported the ideas using the balance scale visual, they then disagree on which side has evidence and reasoning that weighs more than the other. Noe eventually gets convinced that the Panama route is better, but he didn't have to. Notice that they referred to the text in Line 17 and used the visual organizer to organize their ideas according to their pushing down or pushing up (strong points or weak points of the evidence). They also put themselves in the shoes of historical people faced with the same decision.

FIFTH-GRADE LANGUAGE ARTS

Before this lesson, students had read "Learning the Game," a story by Francisco Jimenez (1997) that has parallels between two bullies, an older boy who excludes a younger friend from playing a game, and a boss that demeans a coworker of Francisco's by having the coworker pull a plow. The teacher wanted students to work on skills of building an idea in their conversations, supporting it with evidence, and explaining how the evidence supports it. She used hand motions to help students remember these three key parts of making an argument. Look for conversation skills and different thinking skills. Do students challenge themselves and one another to use clear language and strong ideas? Also watch for when the teacher intervenes. Did her intervention help the conversation?

(1) Teacher: Remember the last story we read with the caterpillar and how Francisco changed. In your conversations I want you to think about themes that are based on comparisons. And the title, this title is "Learning the Game" by Francisco Jimenez. Remember that authors include things for a reason, and they love to put in symbols and metaphors to teach us themes and lessons. Our focal skill for today is fortifying ideas with evidence. (She puts one hand under her other hand making a fist.) But we also want to use skills from the last two days, such as making a claim (fist out and down), and explaining them (hands up to face). Begin.

(2) Ixchel: I think we need to talk about the game, and how Carlos makes up rules, and about Gabriel and the fight and Francisco and the game.

(3) Ismael: They're like each other.

(4) Ixchel: What do you mean?

(5) Ismael: Carlos makes his rules. Not fair. Diaz makes Gabriel pull a plow. That not fair. And he fired him. Also not fair.

(6) Ixchel: Oh. OK. Diaz makes his own rules, like Carlos in the game. So it's like rules of life, but they are bad. And Francisco stands up to Carlos, like Gabriel did to Diaz. So the theme?

(7) Ismael: The theme maybe is not follow rules if not fair.

(8) Ixchel: Not just games, I think. Life, too. Like Gabriel wasn't in a game. He was working. I don't know if/

(9) Ismael: /So the game is life, and you don't follow rules if not fair. That's mine. What's your theme?

(10) Ixchel: That's my theme, too!

(11) Teacher: If you both built the theme, you both can own it. But remember that you need to work together to make it strong and clear to others. You need to use evidence and explain it clearly to others.

(12) Ixchel: So we have to do the hands, claim (fist out and down), support (hand under fist), and explain it (hands to face).

(13) Ismael: OK. Evidence. Francisco don't play the game cuz the rule that Manuelito . . . no puede jugar (can't play).

(14) Ixchel: And evidence is Gabriel breaks Diaz rules. I think he was right. Then Francisco learns to break bad rules. And it's like that word (Ixchel looks at vocabulary chart on wall): boycott. All his brothers stop playing, and Carlos can't play.

(15) Ismael: But Gabriel? He gets fired. He/

(16) Ixchel: /Maybe he comes back and wins, like a movie.

(17) Ismael: It's not a movie. It happened, and I think it's more real. Like in history things aren't fair, and bad people win.

Notice all the thinking and language in this conversation. The two were looking at two examples of evidence, one that was a literal game and one that was more figurative. They had to compare the two and use them to support their theme of not following rules if they aren't fair. There was also plenty of clarification, a use of a key word, *boycott*, and even the beginnings of a critical look at how movies don't always portray the injustices of real life (Line 17). We doubt if this much thinking and language would have happened in their minds if they had just been asked to answer questions or write a written response. And notice how Ismael's final turn might be a foundational idea for future conversations in English language arts classes, history classes, and life.

EIGHTH-GRADE SCIENCE

The lesson focus was on two Next Generation Science Standards: (1) construct, use, and present oral and written arguments supported by empirical evidence and scientific reasoning to support or refute an explanation or a model for a phenomenon (MS-PS3-5) and (2) when two objects interact, each one exerts a force on the other that can cause energy to be transferred to or from the object (MS-PS3-2). There is also the 2012 WIDA ELD Standard 4 for Grade 8: Students at all levels of English language proficiency will ANALYZE energy transfer.

Students have been designing a theme park ride, called FreeFall, which drops people from 100 meters up and then harnesses the energy in some way. The conversation is about the limitations of the models, outside forces that will skew their numbers, the challenges that exist, and what modifications they might need to overcome each challenge.

(1) Teacher: Conversations are a vital part of science, engineering, and design. They help you to clarify and support your ideas; they help you see things you might miss—things that might save lives, in this case. So let's get your conversation muscles warmed up. I want you to talk about the advantages and limitations of the features of your ride design. Remember, *feature* means a part of your design, like a parachute system, and *advantage* is something positive about it. *Limitation* is a weakness in the feature. Take out your constructive conversation skills mini posters we have been using. Today we will focus on fortifying ideas, with some negotiating, especially if you disagree or challenge someone's idea. So, Sara, will you help me model? First, we need a reason to talk. In this case we will talk about which features are the most important for conserving energy in the design of the ride. What do you think is the most important?

(2) Sara: Rollers for electricity.

(3) Teacher: Can you clarify that idea for me?

(4) Sara: Rollers touch the frame on the way down and generate electricity. It's stored in a battery.

(5) Teacher: How can you support this idea?

(6) Sara: We have the numbers from our model. It slows the cage down, but it changed the motion energy into electricity.

(7) Teacher: Hmmm. And you could have it adjust, so it slows the cage all the way to a stop. That way you get as much energy as you can, and you stop the car, so it doesn't crash. Do you think you can capture all the energy?

(8) Sara: Not all the energy. A lot probly changes into heat and sound and wind resistance, too.

(9) Teacher: Interesting! (to whole class) Did you notice how I built on and strengthened Sara's idea? I had a different idea, but I waited and helped her build her idea first. All right. You just saw a sample conversation that focused on building ideas. And even when you challenge an idea, this can help to build it up. Now you will form new teams of two vice presidents of the amusement park company. You are deciding which features should go into the new ride. You have the list we made up here to work with along with the models around the class. I will be looking for how well you build ideas and how well you explain the energy transfers happening during the ride.

I included this conversation to show you how a teacher can set up and model conversation skills. Notice that the teacher first explains the reasons for improving conversation skills in science. The teacher has students take on real-world-like roles to explain, evaluate, negotiate, and choose the design features proposed by the teams. The teacher frames the modeled conversation by describing the things that he wanted to emphasize in the paired conversations, one of which follows. Look for ways in which the students benefitted from the model and practiced some of the target conversation skills and content learning.

(1) Paty: Our feature is a big rubber band, like bungee cord.

(2) Amy: My idea feature is a generator, like when it falls, it makes electricity.

(3) Teacher: Amy, remember to build up, clarify, or respectfully challenge the first idea mentioned by Paty.

(4) Amy: Oh yeah. So, why did you pick the big rubber band?

(5) Paty: It's not. It doesn't cost a lot of money. And it slows it down. Then/

(6) Amy: /How does it save energy? Does it bounce?

(7) Paty: No. At the bottom, a thingy grabs the box and holds it. The rubber band is stretched. Then people get off, and new ones get on. Then unlock it, and it goes up.

(8) Amy: But do they fly up, like when you shoot a rubber band?

(9) Paty: No, but that might be fun. Some gear thing slows it down on the way up.

(10) Amy: So what about the energy transfer?

(11) Paty: Top is potential, then falls, it moves, is kinetic, then hits the bottom and stops, potential, but its elastic potential, not like gravity potential, then kinetic when we let go again. And your idea?

(12) Amy: The generator makes electricity as the box falls. The wheels turn and turn it into electricity.

(13) Paty: What do you do with the electricity?

(14) Amy: Charge batteries.

(15) Paty: Then?

(16) Amy: Use it to send the box back up. And for lights.

(17) Paty: What about the transfer?

(18) Amy: The top is potential, like you said. Then it falls. That's kinetic. And it changes into electricity. That's, I don't know. . . . Mr. E., is electricity kinetic or potential?

(19) Teacher: Electrons are moving through wires, so/

(20) Paty: /Kinetic.

(21) Amy: Then it goes to batteries. That's potential chemical, right? Batteries turn into kinetic to move the box back up.

(22) Teacher: So, which of the two designs is more energy efficient?

(23) Paty: Mine.

(24) Amy: Mine.

(25) Teacher: What can you two do, now, to decide, beyond just saying "mine"?

(26) Amy: Why do you think yours is better for energy?

(27) Paty: Because it doesn't have as many times to change. The book said something like each time you transform it, you lose some. I think cuz of friction. The rubber band just transforms it two times, like from falling to the stored at the bottom in the rubber band and back up from stored to moving it back up.

(28) Amy: OK, my idea transforms it once, from the falling to the wheels, then twice, from the wheels to the generator, then three times, from the generator to the battery, then four times, from the battery back to moving the box back up. Maybe you're right.

In Line 3 the teacher has to remind Amy to build the first idea proposed by Paty. Ideally, we want students to do this without the teacher. Language wise, the students did use key terms such as *transform*, *potential*, and *kinetic* but could have used more complete and more sentences in several turns. Skills wise, Amy and Paty built both ideas without challenging either idea very much, until the teacher asked them to decide which design was more energy efficient in Line 25. Then the two students did a nice job analyzing the features, counting energy transformations, and referring to the book to evaluate and compare the two designs.

NINTH-GRADE ALGEBRA

Students are working on interpreting word problems and solving them in more than one way. This problem is: *Your car is traveling behind another car. You are both going 30 miles an hour. You remember that there is a two-second safety rule that states that you should be 2 seconds behind another car. How far away should you be? How about when you are going 60 mph? How about when going n mph?*

(1)	Teacher:	OK, now I want you converse about this problem and justify the ideas that you have for solving it. I want you to come up with two different ways to solve it, and if there is time, talk about the connections between the two methods. Ready? Go.
(2)	Amit:	What we need to find?
(3)	David:	The most close a car can be when it goes 30 mph.
(4)	Amit:	And 60 and n, too.
(5)	David:	OK, yeah. We gotta be 2 seconds behind, so how far is that?
(6)	Amit:	That's what we gotta find.
(7)	David:	So we're going 30 miles per hour. But we can't use miles.
(8)	Amit:	Why?
(9)	David:	Cuz they're too long. We gotta do feet.
(10)	Amit:	OK. There's like (looks up at wall) 5,280 feet in a mile.

(11) David: OK, we're going 30 miles per hour; that's a lot of feet. Multiply, I think. 30 x 5,280 feet in a mile—that's 158,400 feet per hour.

(12) Amit: Now get it into seconds.

(13) David: Why?

(14) Amit: Cuz it's the 2-second rule, right?

(15) David: Oh, yeah. A hour is 60 minutes, so times 60 seconds is 3,600.

(16) Amit: Now what? We got 158,400 and 3,600.

(17) David: That's feet and seconds.

(18) Amit: So? That's not the answer.

(19) David: I don't know. I don't wanna multiply cuz it's too big.

(20) Amit: So, divide? That's 44.

(21) David: Forty-four what?

(22) Amit: OK. Forty-four feet in a second, I think.

(23) David: That seems right. So in 2 seconds that's 88 feet. Seems right. But my dad drives way closer than that.

(24) Amit: And for 60 you double it, right? From taking 30 and doubling it. You get 176 feet. But for any speed, n, I don't know. Maybe we can/

(25) David: /Make a data table, maybe, like we did last week. 30 gets you 88; 60 gets you 176.

(26) Amit: That's a line, I think. So we find a formula for the line, and that's it.

Notice in this conversation the many turns that students take without either partner dominating the conversation. They ask the important why question in Lines 9 and 13 to draw more reasoning and justification into the conversation. In Line 19 David uses the reasoning that the number would end up being too big if they multiplied. They didn't, however, see how to use the units to help them decide what to do; it was mostly trial and error. We would have liked, in Line 21 for David to ask something like "Even though dividing gets an answer that looks about right, why should we divide here?" How would a mathematician describe this rationale? This is a reminder that we must push our students to push themselves to be as clear as possible in every turn in a conversation.

TENTH-GRADE ENGLISH

Students had read *Fahrenheit 451* by Ray Bradbury, a novel about a futuristic dystopia in which the main character burns books and people are not encouraged to think for themselves or question any decisions made by the government. Students were prompted to bring up and discuss what they thought was its most important theme. Focal standards were (1) cite strong and thorough textual evidence to support analysis of what the text says explicitly as well as inferences drawn from the text (CCSS.RL.9-10.1) and (2) determine a theme or central idea of a text and analyze in detail its development over the course of the text (CCSS.RL.9-10.2).

(1)	Teacher:	I want you all, in pairs, to build a strong theme that you think is the most important for us today. Remember to use evidence from the book and from our lives today.
(2)	Ramon:	So what are we supposed to do?
(3)	Kim:	Come up with a strong theme from this book.
(4)	Ramon:	OK, what about the government that burned all the books?
(5)	Kim:	Yeah. That's what they did, but what's a theme about it? It's not like "Don't burn books."
(6)	Ramon:	OK. So maybe it's "Don't let the government control over too much."
(7)	Kim:	What do you mean?
(8)	Ramon:	In the book, Montag . . . the government burns all books and controls TV shows. But why?

(9) Kim: Maybe it's so the people don't fight against the government. Government thinks that smart people see the bad stuff in government.

(10) Ramon: But that creates stupid people, right? You burn all the books. They don't learn nothing.

(11) Kim: Yeah, but that's what they want.

(12) Ramon: Why?

(13) Kim: Stupid people don't question the government. If they read about stuff like spending lots of money on war, they might complain, maybe even fight.

(14) Ramon: Yeah, in history class lots of people fight up against bad governments.

(15) Kim: Like who?

(16) Ramon: Like the United States. It fought back England, and Mexico fought Spain. If people don't read about stuff like this, they don't get ideas to fight.

(17) Kim: Yeah, like that quote about if they stay entertained, they don't complain. Here it is. "Peace, Montag. Give the people contests they win by remembering the words to more popular songs or the names of state capitals or how much corn Iowa grew last year. Cram them full of noncombustible data, chock them so damned full of 'facts" they feel stuffed but absolutely 'brilliant' with information. Then they'll think they're thinking; they'll get a sense of motion without moving. And they'll be happy because facts of that sort don't change. Don't give them any slippery stuff like philosophy or sociology to tie things up with."

(18) Ramon: How does that help our theme?

(19) Kim: Well, the part where it says, "They'll think they're thinking" and that they will be happy because facts like that don't change. It's like the

government keeps them from really thinking, like thinking about how the government is working. In the book the government was going to war.

(20) Ramon: Like Montag's wife was just watching soap opera walls all day. She and her friends didn't think much. There wasn't any news programs.

(21) Kim: And all the books getting burned. I wonder if it was the stuff in the stories or maybe the fact that people would think they are smart.

(22) Ramon: The government worries 'bout people who think they're smart.

(23) Kim: But not about people crammed with "noncombustible data." What's that?

(24) Ramon: Maybe it's like Facebook. You know, people spend lots of hours on all that stuff that people share. It fills your head and doesn't let you think 'bout bigger problems. Like they don't think about the government and war.

(25) Kim: But the government doesn't control Facebook. And people say bad things about the government sometimes on it.

(26) Kim: Maybe it does control it. We don't know. Maybe it likes Facebook. Cuz it keeps people so busy on computers, they don't get together to do anything more than just keep complaining on Facebook.

(27) Ramon: So for the theme we say that we need to watch out for . . . or how government controls us, like what we think.

(28) Kim: But it's not just what the government does. It's what we do, too. We can't just fill our heads with junk, like Montag's wife. We need to think about important things, like in the government.

(29) Ramon: I like it.

Much of this conversation is spent on clarification and development of a theme and includes a fair amount of supporting this idea with evidence. Notice how the theme evolves from "Don't let the government control over too much" to "We need to think about important things" and taking personal responsibility for what goes into our minds. The conversation allowed this idea to emerge and grow. The students also do a nice job sticking to the text throughout the conversation, analyzing and using a powerful quotation (Line 17), and referring to real-world examples such as Facebook and what they are learning in history class.

ELEVENTH-GRADE HISTORY

Students read primary source documents about the military participation of Navajo soldiers in World War II. Focal standards include (1) analyze how a complex primary source is structured, including how key sentences, paragraphs, and larger portions of the text contribute to the whole (CCSS.RH.11-12.5) and (2) determine the central ideas or information of a primary or secondary source; provide an accurate summary that makes clear the relationships among the key details and ideas (CCSS.RH.11-12.2). The conversation objective is being able to better interpret the language of primary sources for historical purposes, cite evidence, and negotiate differing interpretations with peers.

(1) Teacher: OK. Remember that we are conversing with partners as historians; we are building and comparing ideas and making historical claims based on evidence. Today we will focus on citing evidence to support ideas and negotiating ideas when we disagree. First, historians always have a purpose for looking at a primary source. In this case, we are historians who are deciding if the story of the Code Talkers should be included in the history textbook. We will use a short excerpt from Philip Johnson's *Proposed Plan for Recruiting Indian Signal Personnel.* Now work with a partner. (Pairs form.)

(2) Jose: So should they be in the book?

(3) Aesha: I don't know. Maybe.

(4) Jose: Why maybe?

(5) Aesha: Cuz there's a movie 'bout 'em.

(6) Jose: Yeah, I guess, but why'd they make a movie?

(7) Aesha: Cuz maybe it's a good story.

(8) Jose: They sometimes make up stuff to make it sell, you know.

(9) Aesha: I know.

(10) Jose: So, what now?

(11) Aesha: We decide if it should be in books.

(12) Teacher: Think about what makes an event or person important to learn about. Think about if it hadn't happened, what would have resulted?

(13) Jose: It helped win the war, right? That's important. It was a big war.

(14) Aesha: What if we lost it? Things can be different now.

(15) Jose: How?

(16) Aesha: I don't know. Like maybe Japan can be over everyone.

(17) Jose: Yeah. But I also think that idea of Sara, she shared, about forgiveness. I like it—you know, how they were moved to bad land, like moved from homes and good land, their land. And then the same government asks them for help. I wouldn't have done it. I'd a told 'em to go you know what.

(18) Aesha: Yeah, it shows how good they are to help people who were bad to them.

(19) Jose: They should get their land back, 'specially after helping win that war/

(20) Aesha: /But they didn't help for that. It was to help us cuz they're nice people.

(21) Jose: Maybe they didn't want Japan to take over, and they get moved again.

(22) Teacher: I heard a lot of great conversations. You were all actively engaged. You were using your primary source guides to keep your deep conversations going. Now, let's self-assess with fist-to-five. Remember to hold up five fingers if you did what I say consistently and on down to just a fist, which means you didn't do this at all. Ready? How well did you do taking turns talking? How well did you support your ideas with examples from the text? How well did you build on your partner's ideas? How well did you clarify ideas? How well did you negotiate your ideas? I am impressed that most of you were between a three and a five most of the time. I did notice lower numbers on clarifying, so we can work on that.

The teacher gives his student historians a real-ish purpose (deciding whether or not to include something in a history book) for analyzing primary sources and to guide the conversations. This conversation is not stellar, but it does have several strengths and weaknesses that we can analyze and learn from. For example, they start off talking about a movie as evidence for including it. The explanation in Line 7 was that it "was a good story," but next time they could spend more time talking about the insight in Line 8 about biases that often influence the writing of films. We see some clarification moves in Lines 4, 15, and 20 as well as some use of evidence in Lines 16 and 17. In Line 12 the teacher helps bring them back to thinking like historians. They do some interesting hypothesizing about what might have happened without the Code Talkers, yet they don't include much elaboration or evidential support. In the end in Line 17 Jose offers a long description of an idea brought up earlier by another student about the theme of forgiveness, which provides a theme-based reason for including the Code Talkers in history books in addition to the more cause–effect-based reason of helping the United States win the war. The teacher reinforces conversation skills with a short, kinesthetic, formative self-assessment at the end.

CONCLUSION

As you can see, a lot happens in conversations between students in all grade levels. And these were just samples of one pair of students at one moment in time in a lesson. Many other pairs were conversing at the same time. Consider the wealth of information and insights that you can gain from these types of conversations between students. The challenge, of course, is assessing this talk as a dozen or more conversations happen at the same time. This is the topic of the next chapter.

CHAPTER FIVE

Assessing Conversational Discourse

(1) Yesenia: Those companies hire women and kids, so yeah, that's good.

(2) Ketut: Maybe the jobs for women, but I don't think kids should work.

(3) Yesenia: Why not? They bring money to families to help them survive.

(4) Ketut: If they work, they can't go to school.

(5) Yesenia: But they might go hungry, like, without the money.

(6) Ketut: But those jobs are dangerous, too. Kids get hurt. It said that in the article, like, kids in the rock jobs in South America.

(7) Yesenia: Yeah, but they need to eat. I don't know. Maybe the companies can be watched, and maybe have only half day of work, then maybe they can go to school.

(8) Ketut: That might work, but I don't know how much companies care about kids.

Assessing conversations is both extremely rewarding and highly challenging. Just look at the conversation between Yesenia and Ketut. You might think it is "good" overall, or that it has good and not-so-good parts within it, or you just aren't sure. Conversations vary widely by content area, topic, prompt, partner, preparation, and time. Two students might have very different conversations on the same topic just an hour apart. So what can we do? Well, we often have a sense of what a good conversation is when we hear it. We have already seen quite a few conversations and descriptions of conversation skills in previous chapters of this book. So we can do some assessment and evaluation of conversations, especially if we look at multiple conversations.

But first, what can we learn from analyzing conversations? The following list of benefits might help to convince you—or your colleagues—that assessing conversations is well worth the extra challenges involved.

- **Conversation skills.** First off, we can see how well a student works with another student to build ideas that we want them to build in our classes. Skills that are vital for building ideas include clarifying (and knowing when to prompt for clarification), supporting (and knowing when to prompt for support), comparing, evaluating, and negotiating ideas. All of these, of course, depend in large part on each student's ability to effectively listen to what a partner says.
- **Oral language skills**. Within each turn we can see how well a student articulates his or her thoughts orally. We can see how well a student uses appropriate vocabulary, combines and connects sentences, and uses facial expressions, gestures, and prosody to express ideas within the conversation.
- **Perspectives and connections**. Conversations also offer precious insights into the various views that our students have on life. We can hear their range of perspectives on an issue or the solutions that students propose, many of which we haven't considered. And we can see the connections that they make to their backgrounds and experiences beyond school, all of which can contribute to rich exchanges and building of ideas in a classroom.
- **Classroom culture.** We can observe conversations to see which voices dominate and how they do so. Some students

can hog the airtime, raise their voices, and criticize others to control or dominate the discourse. We can see if participation is equitable, or if there are patterns influenced by race, gender, ELL, or other factors. We can see which students are quiet and which students work well with some or all other students.

- **Content understandings and thinking skills**. We can also learn a lot about the content that students are learning. We can see where students are along the continuum of understanding of complex concepts. We can see how well a student is using the thinking skill(s) that are emphasized in the lesson or unit.

Despite the challenges of assessing conversations, the benefits are worth the effort. You could even do a "cost-benefit analysis" of using conversation as an assessment, in which you would see that for the "cost" of one analyzed conversation, you get multiple key insights in return—and for two or more students at once (Singer & Zwiers, 2016)! Also notice that we put content last on the list of benefits. We did this because content is usually the first thing that teachers want to see, and yet, as we reflect on the other benefits, we see that (1) they are just as or more important than content for succeeding in life and (2) they are vital foundations for rich and lasting learning of content.

How Can We Assess Conversations?

In this section we provide some sample lists and tools that are based on the ideas presented in earlier chapters of this book. However, we will leave it up to you to create your own set of custom tools for observing and assessing student conversations. Some people try to make a grand master tool that covers everything, but there are actually too many important things to look for and evaluate in one conversation. Therefore, you need to choose what is most important for any given time, content, and group of students. What follows is a set of categories and features that you can choose from to create your tailor-made assessment tool. We provide a sample, which might help a little, but what you design in collaboration with colleagues and students will be much more effective.

Options for Creating Conversation Assessment Tools

Conversation skills

Students:

- Create, generate, pose relevant and useful idea(s) to talk about; stick to the prompt.
- Clarify and know when to prompt for clarification.
- Support ideas with evidence and reasoning, and know when to prompt for support.
- Compare and evaluate the strength of ideas.
- Negotiate and challenge ideas.
- Build on ideas; refer to relevant known and given information, and add appropriate new information.
- Take equitable turns.
- Listen.

Maxims and Dispositions

Students:

- Contribute not more or less information than is required at the current stage of the conversation.
- Don't say ideas that they think are false or ideas that lack evidence.
- Try to be as clear as they can.
- Stay relevant to the current stage of the conversation.
- Help partners think more deeply about the topic.
- Allow partners to help each other think more deeply about this topic.
- Come to understand this topic better during conversation.
- Work with partners, not against, even if they disagree at times.
- Remain open to learning new ideas and having ideas change during conversation.

Oral Language Skills

Students:

- Use appropriate vocabulary.
- Combine and connect complete sentences.
- Use pronunciation, intonation, and prosody.
- Use facial expressions, posture, and gestures.

Content Understandings and Thinking Skills

Students:

- Understand the target concept(s) of the lesson or unit, or use and/or allow the conversation to increase content understanding.
- Use the target disciplinary thinking skill(s).
    - *English Language Arts:* Interpret, support an argument, evaluate, apply, synthesize.
    - *History and Social Studies:* Interpret, identify causes and effects, recognize bias, support an argument, evaluate, apply, synthesize.
    - *Science:* Interpret, identify causes and effects, identify variables, support an argument, solve problems, apply, synthesize.
    - *Math:* Interpret, justify ideas with reasoning, solve problems multiple ways, evaluate, apply, synthesize.

Conversation Quality, Conditions, and Support

Teacher:

- Creates an engaging purpose for talking
- Sets up conversations so that each student has information, ideas, or opinions that partners don't know yet (information gap)
- Provides language support to help students communicate as needed
- Provides sufficient modeling, scaffolding, and time for productive and extended talk
- Supports a classroom environment in which students feel safe in sharing their ideas with others
- Helps students value conversation as a way to learn
- Chooses, designs, or adapts curriculum to depend on and leverage conversations for learning

That's a lot of things to assess in one conversation between two students! Moreover, if you try to create rubrics with multiple levels and descriptors for each item, it gets even more complex. It helps to keep any assessment tool as simple as possible, given the already dynamic and complex nature of listening to student conversations. So we recommend choosing a few items from the options for creating conversation assessment tools: items that (1) you think are the most important for your students to learn right now and (2) your students need to work on the most.

Sample Assessment Tool: Second Grade

Here is a sample assessment tool for use in second grade. The teacher who created this purposefully made it generic for use across content areas.

Sample Conversation Assessment Tool for Second Grade

Students:

- Stick to the prompt
- Listen and build on ideas of partners
- Take equitable turns
- Clarify ideas by asking for elaboration and by paraphrasing
- Support ideas with examples from the text
- Work *with* partners, not against, even if they disagree at times
- Use facial expressions, posture, and gestures
- Understand the target concept(s) of the lesson/unit

Let's practice using this sample tool with a snippet of a second-grade conversation. Students read *Once Upon a Time* (Daly, 2004). The teacher asked them to talk in pairs about what they thought the author was trying to teach readers.

(1) Maricela: Maybe not be bullies.

(2) Leila: They were mean to Sarie cuando leía (when she read).

(3) Maricela: Yeah, but we already know that. Bullies are bad. I think to work really hard.

(4) Leila: What do you mean?

(5) Maricela: She didn't go fight them. That doesn't help her read better.

(6) Leila: She practice with her Auntie Anna.

(7) Maricela: Yeah, for a week.

(8) Leila: So she work hard to read good.

(9) Maricela: Yeah. And then she did it.

(10) Leila: Did what?

(11) Maricela: She read beautiful, the principal said.

The teacher could check most of the boxes in the sample tool, even based on this short, transcribed snippet of conversation. The tool would then show that these second graders are building a solid foundation of conversation skills and dispositions to prepare them for future conversation-based learning. If the teacher wanted to gather even more information, she could put evaluative numbers (1, 2, 3) to each box and/or add written observation notes next to them. This would help her provide more feedback to students and inform instruction.

SAMPLE ASSESSMENT TOOL: SEVENTH-GRADE HISTORY

Here is a sample assessment tool used by a seventh-grade history teacher. Notice that it also has a teacher component so that he can reflect on his teaching and support during and after the lesson.

Sample Conversation Assessment Tool for Seventh-Grade History		
Students . . .	**Strengths**	**Needs**
Stick to the prompt.		
Clarify (explain, paraphrase, or define), and prompt partner for clarification.		
Support ideas with evidence from primary sources.		
Negotiate and challenge ideas.		
Build on partner turns.		
Try to be as clear as they can.		
Remain open to learning new ideas and having ideas change during conversation.		

(Continued)

(Continued)

Students . . .	Strengths	Needs
Understand the target concept(s) of the lesson or unit.		
Students use history thinking skill(s): *Interpret primary sources + Identify causes and effects + Recognize biases in sources*		
Teacher—*Did I* . . .		
Create an engaging purpose for talking?		
Provide language support to help students communicate their ideas?		
Provide sufficient modeling and scaffolding?		

Try using the tool with the following conversation about the Spanish conquest of the Aztecs. The prompt was: "Was the Spanish conquest of the Aztecs justified?"

(1) Joel: They shouldn't have invaded the Aztecs.

(2) Samantha: Why not?

(3) Joel: Because they killed them and changed everything.

(4) Samantha: I think it was OK cuz the Aztecs were killing, like sacrifice, lots of people. That's way wrong.

(5) Joel: But you think more killing makes it right?

(6) Samantha: They stopped the sacrifices.

(7) Joel: But I don't think they conquered to stop it. I think they just wanted gold or the land.

(8) Samantha: Why do you think that?

(9) Joel: Cuz it's history. People didn't go across a ocean and fight and conquer to help people. They want gold and land.

(10) Samantha: I still think the people who they will . . . would maybe have been sacrifices got to live. The Spanish helped them.

(11) Joel: Maybe, but not all the rest. Lots died in war and disease and became slaves. Would you want them to come conquer us?

(12) Samantha: No, but we don't sacrifice people.

(13) Joel: Yeah, but the Aztecs could be great Christians. I think the Spanish still will conquer them. They wanted empire.

What strengths and needs would you write down with respect to the rows of the assessment tool? Here's our brief summary. Students did well sticking to the prompt; they didn't clarify enough, although there are several ideas that needed it; and they did support and prompt for support of ideas in Lines 3, 4, 8, and 9. However, they don't refer to primary (or secondary) sources to strengthen their support. In Line 4 Samantha should have continued to help build the first idea posed by Joel rather than posing her opposing idea so quickly. They both build on partner turns, but we don't see much evidence of being open to having their ideas change during the conversation. They seem to understand the concepts of conquest and thinking about it as historians; they also identify causes and effects and even consider hypothetical causes and effects when arguing that the Spanish would have conquered the Aztecs even if they had been devout Christians. Finally, the teacher thought that he created an engaging purpose for talking but didn't provide enough language support. Next time he or she would model and scaffold the use of "would/wouldn't have . . . had/hadn't been . . . even if" to help students pose hypothetical conditions or events.

PEER AND SELF-ASSESSMENT

We can only help students converse to a point, even when they are in our classrooms. It is vital to build in students their abilities to assess the quality of their conversations on their own. You can work with students to build peer and self-assessment tools that are based on the conversation assessment tools that you design, similar to the ones in this chapter. You and students can reword the items to make them more kid friendly, and you can work together to practice using them on sample conversations. One teacher even took videos of student conversations and, with their permission, showed them to the class to practice using the peer assessment tool they had created. This process, as you can imagine, can greatly benefit students in school and beyond. Indeed, we all know adults that don't know that a conversation is going poorly and what to do about it.

SUMMATIVE ASSESSMENT OF CONVERSATIONS

Most of what you have read up until now relates to informal and formative assessment of student conversations. But some teachers have seen a lot of benefits from assessing end-of-semester conversations, similar to other summative writing tasks and tests. Teachers tell students that at the end of the semester, they will be assessed on a conversation about what they have learned with another student in the class. Students know that the many conversations that they have leading up to this assessment will give them a chance to practice the skills and build the dispositions on the assessment tools.

Another type of summative assessment is a teacher-student argument-based conversation, in which you talk with one of your students. The downside is that it is one on one, and therefore time-consuming, especially if you are a secondary teacher with 152 students. The upside is that it is one on one and therefore very informative. You bring up a topic that has two or more competing positions. You more or less follow the collaborative argument model described in Chapter 3. Although it is tempting to ask all the questions and turn it into an interview, you tell the student to facilitate the conversation as much as possible, so you can see how well he or she understands how to have a productive collaborative argument (You can ask, "What should we do next?"). As you engage in conversation with the student, you listen for how well the student describes the issue and works with you to clarify each side and build them up with evidence, evaluate the weight of the evidence on each side to compare them, and come up with a final choice or negotiated conclusion. Ideally, students will have practiced this type of assessment with one another many times beforehand.

CONCLUSION

We may never have perfectly valid and reliable assessments for conversational discourse, but we must continue to assess conversations for several reasons: (1) we continue to learn about students and what they have learned and still need to learn; (2) we learn how to improve our teaching and our own communication skills; and (3) we can provide timely and ongoing feedback that improves students' conversation skills.

CHAPTER SIX

Conclusions, Challenges, and Connections

This book began by connecting the research on academic language and literacy to conversation-based discourse. A framework for how conversational discourse can foster academic language and literacy was presented, along with the essentials of discourse patterns, such as giving up and taking control, paralinguistic clues, and conversation skills. The conversation skills of clarifying ideas, supporting ideas, evaluating evidence and reasoning, negotiating ideas, and competitive argumentation were introduced as well as how to create a classroom culture of collaboration and specific scaffolds for conversation skills.

OVERCOMING CHALLENGES

As discussed in Chapter 1, Think-Pair-Shares and partner talk can be used when first embedding academic oral language into one's classroom, with the eventual goal of developing the conversational skills in this book. Once ELLs, SELs, and their teachers, have become comfortable with integrating academic oral language into their classrooms using structured approaches, they will greatly benefit from moving into conversations that foster higher-order thinking skills (clarifying ideas, supporting ideas, evaluating evidence and reasoning, negotiating ideas, and competitive argumentation).

For many teachers, conversational discourse is an exciting new dimension that can fortify students' learning of content, language, literacy, thinking, and social skills. It provides not only academic benefits but also vital communication skills that go beyond school. Hopefully, this short book has helped you see that we cannot afford not to develop our students' conversation skills if we are to prepare them to have rewarding lives and to sculpt a better world.

Powerful Professional Learning to Enhance ELL and SEL Achievement: Using the Tuning Protocol

To understand and implement the work of this series, we advocate sustained, job-embedded professional learning that is grounded in the work of teacher teams. Reading this book can be a starting place for such learning, and the Tuning Protocol is a tool for self-reflection when analyzing students' conversational discourse.

Specifically, the Tuning Protocol is a powerful design for professional learning that is based on collaborative analysis of student work. Due to the fact that it takes focused professional development over time to change major instructional practices, we recommend that a recursive professional development sequence, like the Tuning Protocol, be used along with the book series. The Tuning Protocol, developed by the Coalition of Essential Schools (Blythe, Allen, & Powell, 1999), can be effective as a way to more deeply explore academic language development strategies and approaches recommended throughout the book series. For example, a department or grade-level team may choose to analyze student work samples from ELLs and/or SELs that address paragraph structures from *Grammar and Syntax in Context* or to analyze the conversational skill of clarifying ideas described in *Conversational Discourse in Context*. A full-cycle collaborative conversation of the Tuning Protocol for conversational discourse is provided here.

THE TUNING PROTOCOL

(1) Presenter describes context of the work to be analyzed (e.g., student level, curriculum, or time allotted).

   Presenter determines focus question, which will be the lens by which the work will be analyzed.

(2) Group silently reviews work and asks clarifying questions only (e.g., How long did it take?).

(3) Group takes notes on warm and cool feedback *regarding the focus question only.*

(4) Group shares warm and cool feedback.

(5) Presenter reflects on next steps for instruction.

(Adapted from Soto, 2012)

TUNING PROTOCOL FOR
THE SKILL OF SUPPORTING IDEAS

In Chapter 3, you read about the skill of supporting ideas. This skill is described as follows:

> using examples, evidence, and reasoning to logically ground or strengthen an idea. This is an essential skill for productive conversations in school, work, and life. Supporting ideas is necessary in most disciplines learned in school. In science, for example, students need to use observed data to support scientific conclusions. In math students must refer to mathematical principles to support a solution method they are using. In language arts students need to use evidence from a story to support an idea for a theme. And in history students need to use evidence from primary sources to support a theory about the main causes or effects of an event.

Once students have discussed and given each other feedback regarding their supporting of ideas, each student can then write down their ideas, and the student work samples can then be analyzed using the Tuning Protocol. For example, using the language arts example, "students need to use evidence from a story to support an idea for a theme," a group of teachers would analyze an individual ELL sample on the skill of supporting ideas, using the five-step Tuning Protocol, as follows:

(1) **Teacher describes the context of the work to the group**— "I taught the skill of supporting ideas after students read the story, *Stellaluna* (the story of a bat who is separated from her mother and raised by birds). In pairs, I had students discuss and come to consensus regarding key quotes from the text that supported the theme of acceptance of differences. My students are in the third grade, and I intentionally paired each ELL with a student whose language was above the ELL's language proficiency level."

   (a) **Presenter determines focus question for analysis of student sample**—The teacher formulates the focus question as her colleagues analyze the student work sample for the skill of supporting ideas. The teacher demonstrates that she would like feedback on how her ELLs can elaborate on their supporting ideas so that they are not merely using one- or two-word responses. The focus question then becomes: "How can I assist my ELLs with elaborating on their supporting ideas?"

(2) **Group reviews work and asks clarifying questions**—One colleague asked the clarifying question: "How did you first introduce the skill of supporting ideas?" The teacher responds, "I reread a segment of *Stellaluna* and provided a think aloud regarding how certain quotes supported the theme of acceptance of differences. I then brought a preselected (and prepared) student up to the front of the class and modeled how to discuss and provide feedback on my evidence." Last, I wrote what we discussed on a piece of paper and under the document reader.

   (a) **Group individually takes notes, highlighting warm and cool feedback**—For warm feedback, participants will analyze the student sample for everything that was done well, from clarifying to using evidence to building on ideas. For cool (not cold) feedback, participants will analyze the student sample according to the focus question only. Recall that the teacher presenter selected the focus question so that he or she is in control of the type of cool feedback that they would like to receive. In this example, the teacher asked for the following cool feedback: "How can I assist my students with elaborating on their supporting ideas?"

(b) **Group shares warm and cool feedback**—One at a time, participants in the group share warm feedback first. It is helpful to use objective frames when providing feedback, such as "I noticed (*for observations*)" and "I wonder *(for questions)*". It is also important to begin with warm feedback as we all want to be viewed from an asset model first. A sample warm feedback statement might be: "*I noticed* that the student's supporting idea accurately supported the theme of acceptance of differences." (Please note that if the Tuning Protocol is being used with a large group, the group facilitator will want to select a few warm and cool feedback statements.) Once the warm feedback has been shared, cool feedback statements can be provided. Recall that cool feedback is based on the focus question only. In this case, the teacher wanted cool feedback regarding the following question: "How can I assist my students with elaborating on their supporting ideas?" A sample cool feedback statement might be: "The student's supporting statement was accurate but could have used additional explanation and justification. *I wonder* if using a sentence frame, so that students have to provide a justification, would assist with elaboration?"

(5) **Presenter reflects on feedback provided**—After all of the warm and cool feedback has been provided, the teacher presenter reflects on his or her next steps from the group discussion of the student work sample on supporting ideas. A sample reflective statement might be: "My next step with teaching supporting ideas will be to model and have students

practice how to elaborate on their supporting ideas by using
a sentence frame for their justification."

We recognize that for many teachers, the ideas in this book and
the book series will require time and practice. Both sustained professional development over time (which can include the Tuning
Protocol) and instructional coaching can be helpful tools. It is also
important for educators to remember to go slow to go fast, that is,
to realize that the strategies and instructional approaches outlined
will take time to approximate. In this manner, just as we honor the
assets of our students, let's honor the assets of our teachers as
excellent learners, who can take on new challenges with appropriate
and sustained professional development over time.

ALD BOOK SERIES SUMMARY
AND INTERSECTIONS ACROSS THE BOOKS

As suggested earlier, the purpose of this four-book series is to
assist educators in developing expertise in, and practical strategies
for, addressing the key dimensions of academic language when
working with ELLs and SELs. In order to systemically address the
needs of ELLs and SELs, we educators must share a common
understanding of academic language development and the inter-
connectedness of its four dimensions.

The following chart provides a summary of the ALD dimension
as well as intersections across the book series. To truly create systemic change for ELLs and SELs in the area of ALD, there must be
a deep understanding of each of the dimensions of ALD under study,
as well as sustained professional development and instructional
efforts to address each dimension, which will be addressed throughout the book series. The book series summary can assist the reader
with where to begin when reading the series, and the intersections
across the book series can assist with making connections as one
completes each book.

This chart allows us to better understand how ALD can and will
support ELLs and SELS to make connections within new rigorous
standards and expectations. Meaningful and intentional planning
around each ALD dimension will allow access for ELLs and SELs

ALD Dimension	Book Series Summary	Intersections Across Book Series
Conversational Discourse	Zwiers and Soto (2016) define *conversational discourse* as the use of language for extended, back-and-forth, and purposeful communication among people. A key feature of conversational discourse is that it is used to create and clarify knowledge, not just transmit it. The essential skills of conversational discourse include the following: • Conversing with a purpose • Clarifying ideas • Supporting ideas and finding evidence • Evaluating evidence and reasoning • Negotiating ideas Successful conversational discourse for ELLs and SELs requires a safe classroom culture and appropriate scaffolds for conversation.	• Conversational discourse necessarily connects to the development of *academic vocabulary* and to its written counterpart, academic writing across genres. • It connects to *grammar and syntax in context* through the need to make and express meaning at the text, paragraph, and sentence levels. • It connects to *culturally and linguistically responsive practices* by engaging students in cooperative practices and respectful listening to other points of view and backgrounds.
Academic Vocabulary	Soto and Calderón (2016) define *academic vocabulary* as a combination of words, phrases, sentences, and strategies to participate in class discussions, to show evidence of understanding and express complex concepts in texts, and to express oneself in academic writing.	• Academic vocabulary, according to Calderón, is the centerpiece of *conversational discourse.* • It connects to *grammar and syntax in context* naturally in that vocabulary is also taught within context. The two dimensions mutually provide meaning for one another.

(Continued)

(Continued)

Academic Vocabulary, continued	To enhance academic vocabulary for ELLs and SELs, teachers select words to specifically teach before, during, and after instruction. They select words and phrases that they believe ELLs and SELs need • to know to comprehend the text. • to discuss those concepts. • to use in their writing later on.	• It connects to *culturally and linguistically responsive practices* in making understandable the distinctions between some common misuses of words ("berry" instead of "very") and the standard English word association.
Grammar and Syntax in Context	According to Freeman, Freeman, and Soto (2016), academic texts pose a particular challenge to ELLs and SELs because they contain technical vocabulary and grammatical structures that are lexically dense and abstract. These include long nominal groups, passives, and complex sentences. ELLs and SELs need carefully scaffolded instruction to write the academic genres, make the writing cohesive, and use appropriate grammatical structures.	• ELLs and SELs need to be engaged in academic discourse to develop their oral academic language. This provides the base for reading and writing academic texts. • ELLs and SELs also need to develop academic vocabulary, both content specific vocabulary and general academic vocabulary that they can use as they read and write the academic genres. • Teachers should use culturally and linguistically responsive practices that enable students to draw on their full linguistic repertoires.

Culturally and Linguistically Responsive Practices	LeMoine cites Gay (2000) in defining *culturally and linguistically responsive practices* as "ways of knowing, understanding, and representing various ethnic groups in teaching academic subjects, processes, and skills." Its primary features benefitting ELLs and SELs include the following: • Promoting cooperation, collaboration, reciprocity, and mutual responsibility for learning • Incorporating high-status, accurate cultural knowledge about different groups of students, and • Cultivating the cultural integrity, individual abilities, and academic success of diverse student groups. Simply stated, it is meaningful learning embedded in language and culture. • Culturally and linguistically responsive practices connect to the development of *academic vocabulary* by providing recognition for prior knowledge and acknowledging culture as part of linguistic development. • It connects to *conversational discourse* by prioritizing cooperative conversation procedures and minimizing confrontational discourse. • It connects to *grammar and syntax in context* by building on second language acquisition strategies and methods (such as SDAIE [Specially Designed Academic Instruction in English] and contrastive analysis).

into content that might otherwise be inaccessible to them. In the Epilogue, you will learn how to use this series in professional development settings and how the book series connects to culturally and linguistically responsive practices.

Epilogue: The Vision

The vision for this book series began with the formation of the Institute for Culturally and Linguistically Responsive Teaching (ICLRT) at Whittier College, the creation of the ICLRT Design Principles, which guides the institute, and the development of an ALD book series, which can assist educators with more deeply meeting the needs of their ELLs and SELs. ICLRT was formed in 2014, and the institute's mission is to "promote relevant research and develop academic resources for ELLs and Standard English Learners (SELs) via linguistically and culturally responsive teaching practices" (ICLRT, n.d.). As such, ICLRT's purpose is to "provide research-based and practitioner-oriented professional development services, tools, and resources for K–12 systems and teacher education programs serving ELLs and SELs." Whittier College is a nationally designated Hispanic-Serving Institution, and ICLRT staff have been providing professional development on ELLs and SELs for more than 15 years, both across California and nationally.

The four books in this ALD series build upon the foundation of the ICLRT Design Principles:

(1) Connecting and addressing the needs of both ELLs and SELs, both linguistically and culturally

(2) Assisting educators with identifying ways to use this book series (and additional ICLRT books) in professional development settings

(3) Addressing the underdeveloped domains of speaking and listening as areas that can be integrated across disciplines and components of ALD

(4) Integrating culturally responsive teaching as a vehicle for honoring both home and primary languages, as well as cultural norms for learning

ICLRT DESIGN PRINCIPLES

Here is a complete list of the ICLRT Design Principles. In parentheses are the books in this series that will address each principle.

(1) **ICLRT believes that the commonalities between ELL and SEL students are more extensive (and more vital to their learning) than the differences between the two groups.**

- ELL and SEL students are at the same end of the learning gap—they often score at the lowest levels on achievement tests. They also rank highly among high school dropouts (*Culture in Context*).
- The academic progress of ELL and SEL students may be hindered by barriers, such as poor identification practices and negative teacher attitudes toward their languages and cultures (*Culture in Context*).
- ELL and SEL students both need specific instructional attention to the development of academic language development (*Grammar and Syntax in Context, Conversational Discourse in Context*, and *Vocabulary in Context*).

(2) **ICLRT believes that ongoing, targeted professional development is the key to redirecting teacher attitudes toward ELL and SEL student groups.**

- Teacher knowledge about the histories and cultures of ELL and SEL students can be addressed through professional development and professional learning communities (*Culture in Context*).
- Teachers will become aware of the origins of nonstandard language usage (*Culture in Context*).
- Teachers can become aware of and comfortable with using diverse texts and productive group work to enhance students' sense of belonging (*Conversational Discourse in Context*).

- The ICLRT Academic Language Certification process will provide local demonstration models of appropriate practices and attitudes (*Conversational Discourse in Context*).

(3) **ICLRT believes that ELL and SEL students need to have ongoing, progressive opportunities for listening and speaking throughout their school experiences.**

- The typical ELD sequence of curriculum and courses do not substantially address ELL and SEL student needs for language development (*Conversational Discourse in Context*, and *Vocabulary in Context*).
- The ICLRT student shadowing protocol and student shadowing app can provide both quantitative and qualitative information about student speaking and listening (*Conversational Discourse in Context*).
- The ICLRT lesson plan design incorporates appropriate speaking and listening development, integrated with reading, writing, and/or content area learning (*Conversational Discourse in Context*).
- Strategies for active listening and academic oral language are embedded in ICLRT's ALD professional development series (*Conversational Discourse in Context*).

(4) **ICLRT believes that its blending of culturally responsive pedagogy (CRP) with ALD will provide teachers of ELL and SEL students with powerful learning tools and strategies.**

- The six characteristics of CRP (Gay, 2000), along with the procedure of contrastive analysis, heighten the already strong effects of solid ALD instruction (*Grammar and Syntax in Context*).
- The storytelling aspects of CRP fit well with the oral language traditions of ELLs, and can be used as a foundational tool for both groups to affirm their rich histories (*Culture in Context*).
- Both groups need specific instruction in the four essential components of ALD, including SDAIE strategies (*Grammar and Syntax in Context, Conversational Discourse in Context*, and *Vocabulary in Context*).

- The inclusion of CRP and ALD within the ICLRT lesson planning tool makes their use seamless, instead of disparate for each group (*Culture in Context*).

Sources: Gay (2000), LeMoine (1999), and Soto-Hinman & Hetzel (2009).

Additional ICLRT Professional Development Resources

This ALD book series is one of the research-based resources developed by ICLRT to assist K–12 systems in serving ELLs and SELs. Other ICLRT resources include the following Corwin texts: *The Literacy Gaps: Building Bridges for ELLs and SELs* (Soto-Hinman & Hetzel, 2009); *ELL Shadowing as a Catalyst for Change* (Soto, 2012); and *Moving From Spoken to Written Language With ELLs* (Soto, 2014). Together, the three books, and their respective professional development modules (available via ICLRT and Corwin), tell a story of how to systemically close achievement gaps with ELLs and SELs by increasing their academic oral language production in academic areas. Specifically, each ICLRT book in the series addresses ALD in the following ways.

- *The Literacy Gaps: Building Bridges for ELLs and SELs* (Soto-Hinman & Hetzel, 2009)—This book is a primer for meeting the literacy needs of ELLs and SELs. Additionally, the linguistic and achievement needs of ELLs and SELs are linked and specific ALD strategies are outlined to comprehensively and coherently meet the needs of both groups of students.
- *ELL Shadowing as a Catalyst for Change* (Soto, 2012)—This book is a way to create urgency around meeting the academic oral language needs of ELLs. Educators shadow an ELL student, guided by the ELL shadowing protocol, which allows them to monitor and collect academic oral language and active listening data. The ethnographic project allows educators to experience a day in the life of an ELL.
- *Moving From Spoken to Written Language With ELLs* (Soto, 2014)—This book assists educators in leveraging spoken language into written language. Specific strategies, such as Think-Pair-Share, the Frayer model, and Reciprocal Teaching, are used to scaffold the writing process, and the Curriculum Cycle (Gibbons, 2002), is recommended as a framework for teaching writing.

Please note that professional development modules for each of the texts listed are also available through ICLRT. For more information, please go to www.whittier.edu/ICLRT.

The ALD book series can be used either after or alongside of *The Literacy Gaps: Building Bridges for ELLs and SELs* (Soto-Hinman & Hetzel, 2009); *ELL Shadowing as a Catalyst for Change* (Soto, 2012); and *Moving From Spoken to Written Language With ELLs* (Soto, 2014) as each book introduces and addresses the importance of ALD for ELLs and SELs. The ALD book series also takes each ALD component deeper by presenting specific research and strategies that will benefit ELLs and SELs in the classroom.

References

Academic Language Development Network. (n.d.). Retrieved from http://aldnetwork.org/

Baker, A., Jensen, P., Kolb, D. (2002). *Conversational learning: An approach to knowledge creation.* Westport, CT: Quorum.

Blythe, T., Allen, D., & Powell, B. S. (1999). *Looking together at student work.* New York: College Teachers Press.

Cazden, C. (2001). *Classroom discourse: The language of teaching and learning.* Portsmouth, NH: Heinemann.

Cisneros, S. (2015). *A house of my own: Stories from my life.* New York: Knopf.

Daly, N. (2004). *Once upon a time.* London: Frances Lincoln Children's Books.

Freeman, D., Freeman, Y., & Soto, I. (2016). *Academic English mastery: Grammar and syntax in context.* Thousand Oaks, CA: Corwin.

Freire, P. (1970). *Pedagogy of the oppressed.* New York: Herder & Herder.

Gadamer, H. G. (1976). *Philosophical hermeneutics.* Berkeley: University of California Press.

Galdone, P. (1985). *The little red hen.* Boston: Houghton Mifflin.

Gay, G. (2000). *Culturally responsive teaching: Theory, research, and practice.* New York: Teachers College Press.

Gibbons, P. (2002). *Scaffolding language, scaffolding learning: Teaching second language learners in the mainstream classroom.* Portsmouth, NH: Heinemann.

Grice, P. (1975). Logic and conversation. In P. Cole & J. Morgan (Eds.), *Syntax and semantics. 3: Speech acts* (pp. 41–58). New York: Academic Press.

Halliday, M., & Matthiessen, C. (2013). *Halliday's introduction to functional grammar* (4th ed.). New York, London.

Institute for Culturally and Linguistically Responsive Teaching (ICLRT). (n.d.). Retrieved from http://www.whittier.edu/ICLRT

Jimenez, F. (1997). Learning the game. In *The Circuit* (pp. 84–95). Albuquerque: University of New Mexico Press.

Krashen, S. (1985). *The input hypothesis: Issues and implications.* London: Longman.

LeMoine, N., & L. A. Unified School District. (1999). *English for your success: A language development program for African American students. Handbook of successful strategies for educators.* Saddle Brook, NJ: The Peoples Publishing Group.

Long, M. H. (1996). The role of the linguistic environment in second language acquisition. In W. Ritchie and T. Bhatia (Eds.), *Handbook of research on language acquisition: Second language acquisition* (pp. 413–468). New York: Academic Press.

Mercer, N. (2000). *The guided construction of knowledge: Talk amongst teachers and learners.* Clevedon, UK: Multilingual Matters.

Migration Policy Institute Tabulation of Data From the United Nations, Department of Economic and Social Affairs. (2013). Trends in international migrant stock: Migrants by origin and destination, 2013 revision (United Nations database, POP/DB/MIG/Stock/Rev.2013). Retrieved from http://esa.un.org/unmigration/TIMSO2013/migrantstocks2013.htm

Singer, T., & Zwiers, J. (2016). Analyzing student conversations as formative data. In *Educational Leadership.* Association for Supervision and Curriculum Development. Retrieved from http://www.ascd.org/publications/educational-leadership/apr16/vol73/num07/What-Conversations-Can-Capture.aspx

Soto, I. (2012). *ELL shadowing as a catalyst for change.* Thousand Oaks, CA: Corwin.

Soto, I. (2014). *From spoken to written language with ELLs.* Thousand Oaks, CA: Corwin.

Soto, I., & Calderón, M. (2016). *Academic English mastery: Vocabulary in context.* Thousand Oaks, CA: Corwin.

Soto-Hinman, I., & Hetzel, J. (2009). *The literacy gaps: Building bridges for ELLs and SELs.* Thousand Oaks, CA: Corwin.

Swain, M. (2000). The output hypothesis and beyond: Mediating acquisition through collaborative dialogue. In J. P. Lantolf (Ed.), *Sociocultural theory and second language learning* (pp. 97–114). New York: Oxford University Press.

Wong-Fillmore, L. (2013). Defining academic language. *Education Week.* Retrieved from http://www.edweek.org/ew/articles/2013/10/30/10cc-academiclanguage.h33.html

Zeldin, T. (1998). *Conversation: How talk can change our lives.* London: The Harvill Press.

Zwiers, J., O'Hara, S., & Pritchard, R. (2014). *Common Core Standards in diverse classrooms: Essential practices for developing academic language and disciplinary literacy.* Portland, ME: Stenhouse.

Index

IS YOUR ACADEMIC LANGUAGE MASTERY LIBRARY COMPLETE?

Academic Language Mastery: Grammar and Syntax in Context
David E. Freeman, Yvonne S. Freeman, and Ivannia Soto

David and Yvonne Freeman shatter the myth that academic language is all about vocabulary, revealing how grammar and syntax inform ELLs' and SELs' grasp of challenging text. Inside you'll find research-backed advice on how to
- Teach grammar in the context of students' speech and writing
- Use strategies such as sentence frames, passives, combining simple sentences into more complex sentences, and nominalization to create more complex noun phrases
- Assess academic language development through a four-step process

Academic Language Mastery: Vocabulary in Context
Margarita Calderón and Ivannia Soto

Vocabulary instruction is not an end in itself. Instead, academic words are best taught as tools for completing and constructing more complex messages. Look to renowned author Margarita Calderón for expert guidelines on how to
- Teach high-frequency academic words and discipline-specific vocabulary across content areas
- Utilize strategies for teaching academic vocabulary, moving students from Tier 1 to Tiers 2 and 3 words and selecting appropriate words to teach
- Assess vocabulary development as you go

Academic Language Mastery: Culture in Context
Noma LeMoine and Ivannia Soto

Never underestimate the critical role culture and language play in our students' education. In this volume, Noma LeMoine offers new insight on how culturally and linguistically responsive pedagogy validates, facilitates, liberates, and empowers our diverse students. Learn how to
- Implement instructional strategies designed to meet the linguistic and cultural needs of ELLs and SELs
- Use language variation as an asset in the classroom
- Recognize and honor prior knowledge, home languages, and cultures

For more information, visit www.corwin.com!

CORWIN
A SAGE Publishing Company

A SAGE Publishing Company

Helping educators make the greatest impact

CORWIN HAS ONE MISSION: to enhance education through intentional professional learning.

We build long-term relationships with our authors, educators, clients, and associations who partner with us to develop and continuously improve the best evidence-based practices that establish and support lifelong learning.

Solutions you want. Experts you trust. Results you need.